Front Cover: The Tay Ninh Provincial Reconnaissance Unit near Nui Ba Den Mountain in 1969. Then-Captain Andrew R. Finlayson, the author of this book, is on the bottom left.

MARINE ADVISORS

WITH THE VIETNAMESE PROVINCIAL RECONNAISSANCE UNITS, 1966-1970

by

Colonel Andrew R. Finlayson

U.S. Marine Corps (Retired)

Occasional Paper

HISTORY DIVISION

UNITED STATES MARINE CORPS

QUANTICO, VIRGINIA

2009

Third Printing

Other Publications in the Occasional Papers Series

Occasional Papers

The History Division has undertaken the publication for limited distribution of various studies, theses, compilations, bibliographies, monographs, and memoirs, as well as proceedings at selected workshops, seminars, symposia, and similar colloquia, which it considers to be of significant value for audiences interested in Marine Corps history. These "Occasional Papers," which are chosen for their intrinsic worth, must reflect structured research, present a contribution to historical knowledge not readily available in published sources, and reflect original content on the part of the author, compiler, or editor. It is the intent of the Division that these occasional papers be distributed to selected institutions, such as service schools, official Department of Defense historical agencies, and directly concerned Marine Corps organizations, so the information contained therein will be available for study and exploitation.

TABLE OF CONTENTS

Preface

U.S. Marines as advisors have a long history, from Presley O'Bannon at Tripoli through Iraq and Afghanistan via Haiti, Dominican Republic, Nicaragua, China, South Korea, Taiwan, Philippines, and Vietnam. While most Marines think of the Vietnamese Marine Corps as the primary advisory experience during that conflict, others served with various other advisory programs with the U.S. Army, U.S. Navy, U.S. Joint Special Operations, and U.S. Civil Operations and Rural Development Support. One of these is the subject of this study: Marine advisors with the Vietnamese Provincial Reconnaissance Units (PRUs). This narrative is a combination of experience, research, and reflection. While other journalistic or academic accounts have been published, this is a narrative of participants.

Many historians consider the two most effective counterinsurgency organizations employed during the Vietnam War to have been the PRU and USMC Combined Action Platoons (CAP). In both cases, U.S. Marines played a significant role in the success of these innovative programs. It should be pointed out, however, that the number of U.S. Marines assigned to these programs was small and the bulk of the forces were locally recruited fighters. Both programs used a small cadre of Marines providing leadership, training, and combat support for large numbers of indigenous troops, and in so doing, capitalized on the inherent strengths of each.

The author believes that both of these programs have applicability in any counterinsurgency where U.S. forces are called upon to assist a host government. Obviously, adjustments to these programs would have to be made to take into account local conditions, but the core concept of providing U.S. Marines to command or advise local militia and special police units is one that has great promise for success. With a clear understanding of why the PRUs and CAPs worked, and with the necessary adjustments to take into account local conditions, similar units can be created to defeat future insurgencies. With this in mind, the author hopes that this work will provide U.S. military planners with insights into creating and managing units capable of defeating a well-organized and highly motivated insurgent political infrastructure.

Acknowledgments

I would like to thank several people who were instrumental in the creation of this work and whose assistance allowed me to overcome many obstacles to acquiring firsthand accounts of U.S. Marines who served as advisors with the Provincial Reconnaissance Unit (PRU) program. First, I would like to thank General James N. Mattis for suggesting that I write this work. General Mattis felt that this book would serve as a means of capturing important counterinsurgency "lessons learned" during the Vietnam War, and in so doing, provide valuable insights for present-day Marines as they fight other insurgencies in other lands.

Second, I wish to express my deep gratitude to Dr. Mark Moyar, the author of the most objective and accurate book concerning the Phoenix program, *Phoenix and the Birds of Prey*. Dr. Moyar was the first historian of note to do the kind of thorough research into the Phoenix program needed to strip away the misunderstandings surrounding this counterinsurgency program. I am indebted to him for his support and insights during the creation of this work.

One individual, Lieutenant Colonel (Ret) George W.T. "Digger" O'Dell, provided invaluable assistance to me by putting me in touch with former Central Intelligence Agency (CIA) officers who had been involved with the PRU and could provide information on how the CIA viewed the contribution of the military assignees to the program. Lieutenant Colonel O'Dell served in the Marine Corps from 1965 to 1968, and then left the Marine Corps to join the CIA as a paramilitary officer in Laos and the Middle East from 1969 to 1975, before returning to the Marine Corps to finish his career in 1992 as one of the Corps' few experts in the area of special warfare. He was tireless in his efforts to introduce me to his many friends in the CIA who had knowledge of the PRU Program.

I was ably assisted with the editing and formatting of this work by two longtime friends and colleagues, Hildegard Bachman and Mary Davisson. They provided many professional and valuable suggestions on how to improve the content and appearance.

I would like to thank several former CIA officers who provided valuable background material on the Phoenix program, the PRUs, and contact information on the Marines who served as advisors. They are Rudy Enders, Ray Lau, Hank Ryan, Warren H. Milberg, William Cervenak, and Charles O. Stainback. These patriots served their country in silence, often in extremely dangerous assignments, and I am both indebted to them for their assistance with this paper and for their unsung service to our nation.

At the History Division, Chief Historian Charles D. Melson provided project guidance, with editing by Kenneth H. Williams and layout and design by W. Stephen Hill.

I also thank *Studies in Intelligence* for permission to reprint the map of Tay Ninh from my 2007 article.

Introduction

During the latter stages of the Vietnam War, small teams of dedicated and courageous Vietnamese special police, led by American military and Central Intelligence Agency (CIA) personnel, fought a largely unsung war against the political leadership of the Communist insurgency. These special police units were called Provincial Reconnaissance Units (PRUs), and they conducted some of the most dangerous and difficult operations of the Vietnam War. Because these units were created, trained, equipped, and managed by the CIA, they worked in secret, a status that often led to myths and falsehoods about their activities. So pervasive are these myths and falsehoods that many historians often take them at face value without subjecting them to the same scrutiny as other historical aspects of the Vietnam War. This lack of understanding is further complicated because of the political divisiveness within the United States surrounding the Vietnam War, which led some opponents of U.S. involvement in that war to accept the most pernicious and false claims made against the entire pacification effort conducted by the American and South Vietnamese governments.

The passage of time and the work of some historians have helped to lift the shroud of secrecy around the PRU and their battle against the Viet Cong.[1] This book relates the story of how a small group of U.S. Marines assigned to this program contributed to the program's success and to identify, using official records, personal interviews, and other unclassified sources the factors that contributed to that success.[2] In so doing, I hope to inform the reader about why the PRU Program was so successful in destroying the Viet Cong Infrastructure (VCI) despite many obstacles placed in its way by both the South Vietnamese and United States governments.

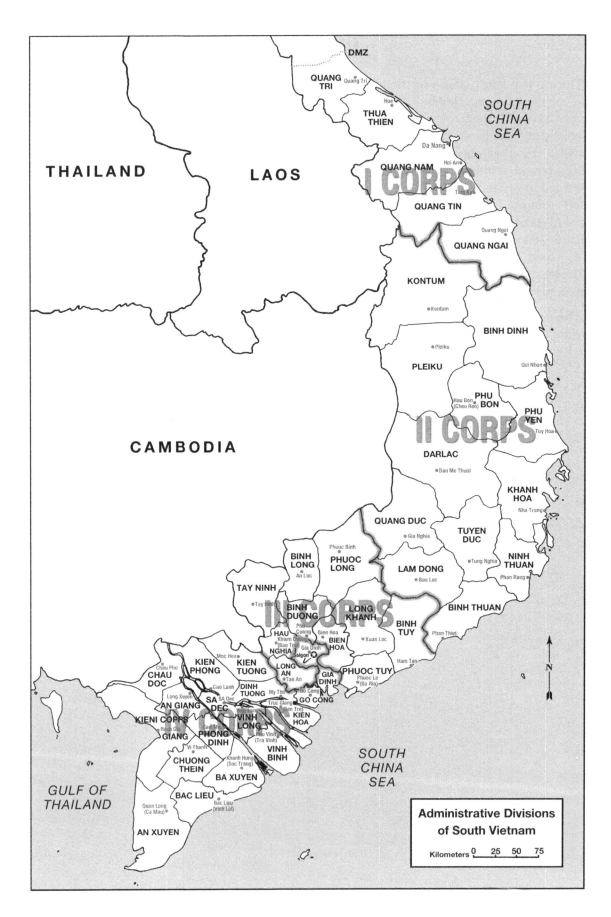

Administrative Divisions of South Vietnam

2

The Beginning

The Vietnam War was really two wars. One was the purely military war pursued by the North Vietnamese Army (NVA) against the military forces of the government of South Vietnam (GVN) and the United States of America. The other war was the insurgency waged by the Viet Cong political apparatus, an extension of the Lao Dong Party in South Vietnam, using local political cadre and guerrillas. These two wars were part of an overall strategy of the North Vietnamese Lao Dong Party to overthrow the GVN and unite all of Indochina, including Laos and Cambodia, under their control. This dual-track strategy by the North Vietnamese Communists modulated between an emphasis on classic Maoist revolutionary war from 1956 to 1968 to a predominantly conventional war strategy from 1968 until the fall of Saigon in 1975.

The scope of this work does not allow for an analysis of the dual-track strategic approach by the North Vietnamese, but an understanding of it is necessary for the reader to comprehend how both sides fought the war. I leave it to the reader to refer to several excellent books on this subject, such as Mark Moyar's *Triumph Forsaken*, Lewis Sorley's *A Better War*, and Harry Summers's *On Strategy*, for analyses of how this strategy was applied during the war. The author's *1988 Marine Corps Gazette* article may also prove helpful.[3]

This work examines one aspect of the counterinsurgency war waged in South Vietnam against the Communist political leadership (hereafter referred to as the Viet Cong Infrastructure, or VCI) of that insurgency. It deals with the primary instrument used by the U.S. Central Intelligence Agency (CIA) to attack and defeat the VCI—the Provincial Reconnaissance Unit (PRU) Program.

Rudy Enders, the legendary chief of operations for the CIA and one of the CIA's most original and effective organizers of paramilitary operations, explains below the origins of the Phoenix program in South Vietnam and the role the PRUs played in the early years of its existence. We pick up his story, in his own words, in 1966:

As Agency-supported programs matured, the volume of intelligence at province level became overwhelming. Some of it was tactical, but most pertained to the VCI. As one would expect, the collector seldom shared exploitable intelligence with anyone. With spies everywhere, who could be trusted? Why should you pass hot information and let others take credit for the operation? This could be said of the National Police, Special Branch, Rural Development Cadre, PRU, Military Security Service, and Sector and Subsector G-2s. In late 1966, they were all running operations against the VCI, but there was little coordination or cooperation. Besides, delays in reaching province often rendered information totally useless. Obviously, something had to be done. The answer was to design a mechanism to ensure cooperation amongst all existing South Vietnamese organizations operating against the VCI, and that this be done at the district as well as the province levels.

The CIA's Region One ROIC [Regional Officer in Charge] and his deputy grabbed the bull by the horns. They decided to run a pilot program in Quang Nam Province's five districts, starting with Dien Ban District. Visits to these districts revealed few had 1:50,000 scale maps of their area, a war room, or any files on VCI cadre. It was shocking. Most district compounds had barely enough room for the subsector staff and advisors. Accordingly, the ROIC asked General [Lewis W.] Walt, the commander of the Marines in I Corps, for supplies to build five A-frame-type wooden District Intelligence and Operation Coordinating Centers (DIOCC). The centers would be staffed by representatives from the CIA's Census Grievance, PRU, Rural Development, and Police Special Branch, along with the South Vietnamese National Police and Military Security Service. They would be run by the district chief's S-2 and advised by an American officer. The ROIC explained his initiative to John Hart, the CIA's Saigon station chief at the time, and he used the term Intelligence Coordination and Exploitation (ICEX) as a way to describe the concept.

Provincial Reconnaissance Unit operators in Thua Thien Province in 1967. In areas contested or controlled by the Vietnamese Communists, they would go on operations dressed to blend in with the Viet Cong (VC) or North Vietnamese Army (NVA). The weapon is a Communist bloc AK-47.

CIA felt ICEX was too much of a mouthful and began looking for a symbolic alternative by holding a region-wide contest to find a new name for the program. The word was passed to all I Corps POICs, and the RDC/P (Rural Development Cadre/Programs) officer in Quang Ngai suggested *Phuong Hoang*, Vietnamese for *Phoenix*, the mythical bird that emerges from ashes. He won the contest, and that is how the Phoenix program got its name.

Phoenix was nothing more than a coordination and exploitation program directed against terrorists and those supporting terrorists. Organizations which came under the Phoenix umbrella were already working against the VCI. The only difference involved sitting down at the table to coordinate and exploit relevant, usable intelligence. It was

not some devious, nefarious CIA plot to assassinate unarmed civilians. Those who risked their lives going after armed terrorists were not murderers. They were legitimate military, paramilitary, and lawful police forces facing terrorists, spies, and nonuniformed armed insurgents. Blaming Phoenix for VCI deaths is like calling the FBI murderers because armed terrorists preferred to fight rather than surrender to lawful authority. . . .

After we established the DIOCCs in I Corps, the Phoenix program began to take on a life of its own. The clandestine VCI became our top priority. As long as it existed, pacification was impossible. VC terror tactics were far more effective in winning over the population than any "hearts and minds" program. ICEX/Phoenix soon came under the microscope of the Saigon Station staff and was eventually scrutinized by the ambassador and Robert "Blowtorch" Komer. It didn't take long for Komer to seize upon Phoenix as a way to make his mark in Vietnam. He had President [Lyndon B.] Johnson's ear and this made him politically powerful. Anyone standing in his way would be run over with a bulldozer.

If anyone could move the program forward, it was this overbearing, arrogant, mission-driven former CIA analyst. He acted as a ramrod to implement a "rifle shot" rather than a "shotgun" approach to the VCI. As the number-three man in Saigon, he vetoed various "concept" papers until a "missions and functions" paper finally appeared before him, which he accepted. "Anything else," he said, "would not be understood by the military."

Although Komer would be the Phoenix "Czar," he needed someone to actually run the program. Here he fingered CIA's Evan Parker Jr. of the Parker Pen Company. He couldn't have made a better choice. Evan Parker was a first-generation paramilitary officer, having served with OSS Detachment 101 during World War II as a liaison officer with Merrill's Marauders and the British. He was a GS-16 at the time, considered highly *intelligent, soft-spoken, well organized, enormously respected, and extremely capable. He also came from my parent Special Operations Division at CIA headquarters and later became its chief, an organization I would later head.*

Essentially, those in Saigon institutionalized what we were already doing in I Corps. By the summer of 1967, MACV agreed to assign military intelligence officers to the DIOCCs and PIOCCs throughout the country. The name change to Phoenix (except in I Corps) was in transition; thus, all the early program guidance written by Parker's staff was circulated as ICEX memoranda. All of this meant nothing to us in I Corps except added focus and high-level attention to what we were doing. Indeed, many of the papers circulated were simply upgraded versions of what we already had drafted to explain ICEX to Saigon.[4]

As Enders stated, the Phoenix program was an effort to unify the disparate counterinsurgency programs of both the United States and the GVN so a more effective approach could be developed. This widely misunderstood program was a bureaucratic consolidation of the various ongoing intelligence-gathering efforts being employed in South Vietnam to fight the Communist political infrastructure. Because the Phoenix program included several CIA-sponsored activities, such as the PRUs, it was given an aura of secrecy that only served to arouse suspicion among many observers and later among some scholars that the program somehow involved "illegal" or "criminal" activities.[5] In reality, the Phoenix program sought to organize the fight against the VCI in a more systematic and effective manner by requiring the various GVN and American agencies to cooperate and coordinate on a countrywide level.

The efficacy of this approach was not lost on the Communists, who recognized and acknowledged the serious threat Phoenix posed to their plans to subvert the GVN. In fact, there is no more cogent proof of the fear that Phoenix instilled in the Communists than the

comments of several North Vietnamese Communists who verified the program's effectiveness after winning the war. Perhaps the most telling of these are credited to Mai Chi Tho, who controlled the most famous Viet Cong spy of the war, Pham Xuan An, a strategically placed journalist in the *Time* magazine office in Saigon. He identified An's "most valuable contribution" over nearly 25 years of spying for the North Vietnamese as "everything on the pacification program . . . so we could develop an 'anti' plan to defeat them. . . . I consider this to be the most important because of its strategic scale."[6]

Despite having the complete American and South Vietnamese pacification plans, the Communists never were able to defeat the GVN pacification program and, indeed, by early 1969, the Communists realized that their plan for a "general uprising" using local Viet Cong units in South Vietnam was doomed to failure and that a purely military solution involving Communist forces from North Vietnam invading South Vietnam was the proper strategy to pursue. Internal Communist documents and information provided by CIA spies within the VCI confirmed that the VCI and their VC guerrilla forces were largely defeated by early 1970 leaving little option for the northern Communists but to pursue a conventional military strategy. For an insight into this changed strategy from the enemy's side, see Truong Nhu Tang's *Viet Cong Memoir*, which details the enemy's analysis of the military and political situation in South Vietnam during the crucial year of 1970.

To understand the PRU Program and how it was used to attack the VCI, it is helpful to understand how it fit into the overall Phoenix program, in theory and practice. Before 1967, the PRU teams were under the control of CIA officers in many of Vietnam's 44 provinces, but they had no real national-level coordination mechanism. It was in 1967 that the PRU finally became a national program under CIA officer Evan Parker and was given its national-level mission of defeating the political infrastructure of the Viet Cong.[7] The ICEX Program evolved into the Phoenix program, but the PRU mission remained the same despite this organizational change.

The Phoenix program as it emerged at the end of 1967 had organizational structures at every level of administration in South Vietnam. At the national level, the Phoenix Committee was chaired by the minister of interior, with the director general of the National Police as the vice chairman. Other members of the national-level Phoenix Committee were the minister of defense, the J-2 and J-3 of the Joint General Staff, and representatives from the National Police Field Force (NPFF), the Police Special Branch (PSB), the Revolutionary Development (RD) Ministry, and the Chieu Hoi Ministry.

At the national level, one of the key CIA assistants to the CIA's chief of station on the PRU Program was the legendary Tucker Gouglemann, a former Marine who was severely wounded during the battle for Guadalcanal. He was medically discharged from the Marine Corps after World War II and joined the CIA. The author had several conversations with Mr. Gouglemann in the Duc Hotel in Saigon in 1969 and found him to be a highly intelligent and engaging man who could best be described as a brilliant and profane curmudgeon who possessed an intense love for his job and the Vietnamese. He also had an almost pathological hatred of bureaucracy and bureaucrats, whom he felt had little understanding of Vietnam or how the war should be fought. Sadly, Gouglemann was captured in Saigon after the Communist victory in 1975 and died undergoing interrogation by the North Vietnamese. His body was released to the American government two years after his capture and showed clear signs of torture.[8]

The senior U.S. Marine officer assigned to the PRU was then-Lieutenant Colonel Terence M. Allen, a combat veteran of the Korean and Vietnam wars who spent nearly three years in Vietnam running the Department of Defense (DoD) side of the PRU program. He was tireless in his efforts to mold the PRU into an effective counter-VCI organization, a task that was often complicated and frustrated by what

he described as "the obstruction of the U.S. State Department and the naïve and false reporting of U.S. journalists who had no valid understanding of the PRU."[9] Major, later Colonel, Nguyen Van Lang was the senior Vietnamese assigned to the PRU headquarters in Saigon. Later, Major Lang became the director of the PRU when control of the PRU passed from the CIA to the South Vietnamese National Police. From 1968 until 1970, Colonel Allen's job involved providing advice and assistance to Major Lang on the national administration of the program.

At the regional level, the Phoenix Committee was chaired by the region's military commander, and the deputy chair was the region's National Police commander. The remainder of the committee was made up of representatives from the same ministries found on the national committee.

The provincial Phoenix Committee differed from the national and regional Phoenix committees in one very significant way. The national and regional Phoenix committees were largely administrative entities that provided guidance and advice to the senior Vietnamese political leaders and set counterinsurgency policy. The provincial Phoenix committees were actively engaged in the collection of intelligence on, and the targeting of, the VCI. The provincial Phoenix committees were chaired by the province chief, normally an ARVN colonel or lieutenant colonel, with the provincial police chief as the deputy-chairman, although in some provinces the cochair was the provincial intelligence officer. Representatives of the G-2, the G-3, the Rural Development (RD) program, the Police Special Branch (PSB), Census Grievance (CG), the National Police Field Force (NPFF), and the Chieu Hoi program made up the rest of the committee, along with intelligence officers from the military units in the province. The provincial Phoenix committees were required to meet at least once a week, but they often met far more frequently, sometimes daily. They operated 24 hours a day, every day, collecting and discussing intelligence on the VCI, maintaining extensive records on the progress of the anti-VCI effort in their province, and issuing arrest orders for VCI suspects.

Below the provincial Phoenix committees were the DIOCCs. These were the district-level Phoenix Committees, and they served as the front-line units in the war on the VCI. The DIOCC was organized along the same lines as the Provincial Phoenix Committee, and like the Provincial Phoenix Committee, it operated 24 hours a day, seven days a week. In addition to its intelligence-gathering and VCI-targeting duties, it also provided intelligence for the American and Vietnamese military units stationed in the district. Each DIOCC had four sections: administrative, military intelligence, police intelligence, and operations. In many DIOCCs, the PRU was represented, but normally they had no representation on the DIOCC. Instead, the PRU provided its intelligence input to the police intelligence representative in the DIOCC and received missions directly from the district chief.[10]

The DIOCCs created dossiers on VCI personnel and coordinated the efforts to arrest VCI and bring them to justice. They also maintained a list of all VCI positions in the district and attempted to identify the individuals in these positions. While many organizations were given the mission of defeating the VCI, such as the National Police, the National Police Special Branch, and the armed forces of the United States and GVN, the principal action arm of the Phoenix committees was the CIA-organized, -funded, and -controlled PRU.

In theory, the DIOCC system provided the infrastructure needed to collect intelligence on the VCI and to coordinate operations against it. In practice, the DIOCC system did not always work as it was intended. According to the U.S. Marine PRU advisors interviewed by the author, the DIOCC system worked very well in the provinces where the representatives of the Vietnamese and American agencies on the various regional, provincial, and district Phoenix committees worked well together and cooperated in the generation of operational leads.

However, several of the Marine PRU advi-

Chart re-created from Andradé, *Ashes to Ashes*, p.291

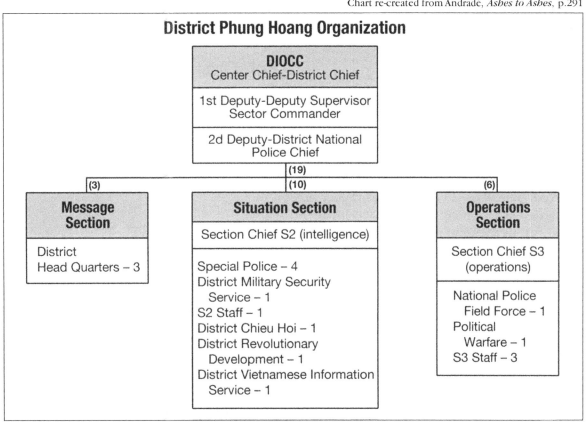

sors interviewed for this paper stated that the system in their province did not meet the standards necessary to fully exploit the DIOCC system. They attributed this situation to several factors, but the primary one was bureaucratic jealousy on the part of the agencies represented on the provincial and district-level Phoenix committees. They also identified a reluctance to share operational leads since the agencies involved were afraid they would not receive the credit (and the budget allocations) they deserved if another agency acted on the intelligence they gathered. Petty personality conflicts also militated against the smooth functioning of many DIOCCs. They stressed that where the provincial and district chiefs had strong leadership skills and where American advisors to the representatives on the DIOCCs enjoyed the confidence and respect of their Vietnamese counterparts, the DIOCCs functioned effectively.

Once the Phoenix program became a nationwide program with an organizational structure that ran from Saigon to each district in the country, the CIA soon realized it did not possess the personnel needed to provide the required advisors for the PRU Program. Indeed, it was having great difficulty finding adequate numbers of CIA case officers for other tasks in South Vietnam, especially case officers with any experience in paramilitary activities such as were required to advise the PRU. Since every province in South Vietnam needed a PRU advisor and in some cases two, the CIA needed at least 44 American provincial PRU advisors and 30 regional and Saigon-based headquarters staff. With a very limited number of CIA paramilitary officers available worldwide, it was readily apparent that the CIA would not be able to provide these PRU advisors using their own personnel.

This serious shortcoming needed to be solved if effective control of the PRU was to be established and maintained by the CIA. The solution to this problem came in the form of assigning U.S. military personnel to the PRU Program using cover orders assigning them to the Combined Studies Division (CSD) of the Military Assistance Command, Vietnam

(MACV). Ideally, these DoD assignees were to be skilled in the special warfare tasks needed by a PRU advisor. With this in mind, the bulk of the PRU advisors came from the U.S. Army's Special Forces, the Navy's Seals, and the U.S. Marine Corps' Force Reconnaissance Companies.

Since it was envisioned that the PRU would have to coordinate closely with and support U.S. forces, it was decided to assign PRU advisors to the four military regions based upon service affiliation. For instance, since the bulk of U.S. forces in I Corps were U.S. Marines, the CIA tried to assign Marine PRU advisors to that military region. The U.S. Army was heavily represented in II Corps and III Corps, so the CIA assigned U.S. Army Special Forces and U.S. Army Military Intelligence PRU advisors to those two military regions. U.S. Navy Seals were assigned as PRU advisors to the southernmost military region, IV Corps. The first large contingent of U.S. military advisors was assigned to the PRU in 1967. However, some U.S. military personnel had been assigned to the PRU in very small numbers before 1967 when the PRU Program was not organized countrywide. Most of these early U.S. military PRU advisors were assigned to I Corps.[11]

PRU Organization, Recruitment, Equipment, and Command and Control

Before 1967, the PRUs existed at the provincial level, and less than half of the provinces in South Vietnam had such units. They ranged in size from 30 to 300 men, depending on the size of the province and the need for their services by the provincial chiefs and the CIA. Many of the early PRU units were organized along strictly military lines since they were often employed in military operations against main force VC units. In 1967, when Civil Operations and Rural Development Support (CORDS) took over operation of the PRU Program, the CIA decided to give the PRU a countrywide presence and a standard table of organization for a PRU team. For reasons that are not known, it was decided that each PRU team would consist of 18 men broken down

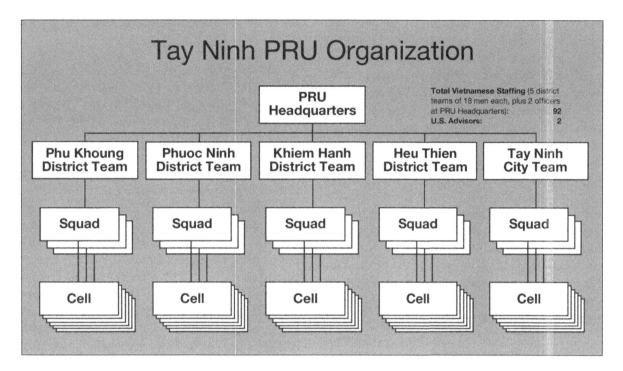

Tay Ninh PRU Organization

PRU Headquarters

Total Vietnamese Staffing (5 district teams of 18 men each, plus 2 officers at PRU Headquarters): 92
U.S. Advisors: 2

| Phu Khoung District Team | Phuoc Ninh District Team | Khiem Hanh District Team | Heu Thien District Team | Tay Ninh City Team |

Squad — Squad — Squad — Squad — Squad

Cell — Cell — Cell — Cell — Cell

into three six-man squads. The senior squad leader in each team became the team leader. The idea was to assign an 18-man PRU team to each district so the team could react quickly to any targets identified by the DIOCC in that district. In theory, each province would be given enough PRU teams for one to be assigned to each DIOCC. This new organization went into effect in late 1967 and was maintained until the PRUs were integrated into the GVN National Police in 1973. This new national-level PRU organization resulted in most districts receiving an 18-man PRU team, which meant that small provinces with only a few districts or no districts had fewer than 50 PRU members assigned while larger, more populous provinces with many districts had as many as 300 PRU members assigned. In total, 4,000 to 6,000 Vietnamese PRU personnel were assigned countrywide to the program during the years 1967 to 1975.[12]

A typical post-1967 provincial PRU organization was the one found in Tay Ninh Province in South Vietnam's III Corps. In this organization, each of the four districts in Tay Ninh Province was assigned an 18-man PRU team and an additional 18-man team was assigned to the capital of the province as a "city team" that could mount operations in the densely populated Tay Ninh City or be used to reinforce one or more of the district teams. A very small headquarters cell consisting of the South Vietnamese PRU commander; his deputy, who was also the leader of the Tay Ninh City PRU team; and an operations/intelligence officer provided the staff planning and interagency coordination for the province. According to the Marines assigned to the PRU, this form of organizational structure worked well despite the paucity of personnel assigned to staff duties.

The recruitment of PRU personnel varied from province to province. Many PRU members were former VC or former ARVN soldiers. Some were former South Vietnamese Special Forces soldiers or former members of a Citizen Irregular Defense Group (CIDG), while a few were simply local youths who did not want to join the regular ARVN forces and preferred to serve their country in their own home province. In a few provinces, some paroled criminals were allowed to join the PRU, but the number of such people was few and greatly reduced after 1968. Some had strong religious and community affiliations that made them natural enemies of the Communists, such as Catholics, Cao Dai, Hoa Hao, and Montagnard tribesmen. Most PRU members were strongly motivated by their hatred of the VCI.[13] Since there were many people in every province who had a grudge against the VCI, there were many South Vietnamese who were eager to join the PRU. The fact that most PRU hated the VCI made them a very formidable force and one that made it very difficult for the Communists to infiltrate or proselytize.[14] According to Colonel Terence M. Allen, the senior military advisor to the PRU Program in Saigon from 1968 to 1970, the most effective PRU teams were those who were recruited among the Cao Dai and Catholic religious communities and the Montagnard tribes since these groups had a visceral hatred of the Viet Cong and a vested interest in protecting their communities from the ravages inflicted on them by the VCI terrorist cells.

The Marine PRU advisors interviewed by the author expressed confidence in the recruiting methods used to obtain PRU members and felt the men assigned to their units were, on balance, extremely competent and experienced. However, there were some notable exceptions. This was especially true in the early phases of the PRU program when MACV first began to assign its personnel in I Corps. The senior CIA officer in Quang Tri Province in 1967, Warren H. Milberg, explained one province's recruiting problem this way:

Quang Tri was a relatively sparsely populated province. By mid-1967, the war was heating up at all levels. Young men of military age and qualification were either in the ARVN, the CIDG, or were engaged in farming in the districts. PRU recruitment became a problem of demographics: there was just not a large pool of physically and mentally qualified young men to choose from. It was pretty well known in the province what the PRU did and what their mission was so that even those who may have otherwise qualified were too risk-averse to want to join. The people we did manage to recruit all came with their own set of "issues." For the most part, this was not a problem, although we did have some exceptions here and there. In the end, they became a great group of brave fighters, but they were not unlike a pack of

pit bulls: training, discipline, leadership and focus were needed all the time.[15]

The experience of PRU advisor Sergeant Rodney H. Pupuhi in 1968 illustrates the recruiting challenges faced by the PRU in I Corps. When he reported to his PRU unit in Hoi An, Quang Nam Province, in March 1968 shortly after the Tet Offensive, he was not encouraged by what he found. The Quang Nam PRU was in the midst of being disbanded, and only seven PRU members remained out of the original pre-Tet force of more than 100 men. Like any good Marine noncommissioned officer, Sergeant Pupuhi immediately took charge of the situation, held a formation of his remaining seven-man PRU force, made them squad leaders, and sent them to their home villages to recruit replacements for each squad. As he put it, "I gave these men strict guidelines on recruiting and a deadline of two weeks to return with enough recruits to fill the seven squads. Slowly, these men came back with 'family within family' recruits—that is, brothers recruited other brothers and nephews recruited cousins until we had the necessary numbers to fill the squads."

Pupuhi arranged with the CIA to give the recruits' families advance pay and to have Air America fly the recruits to Hoi An. In short order, Pupuhi had resurrected the Hoi An PRU with reliable men and had embarked on a rigorous training program to prepare his new recruits for their demanding and dangerous missions. Within six weeks of his arrival in Hoi An, he had recruited, trained, and equipped his new unit and began conducting counter-VCI operations.[16]

PRU teams were equipped with an assortment of uniforms, weapons, and equipment. Most PRU members dressed in the black pajamas worn by Vietnam's peasants or tiger-striped camouflage uniforms when they went to the field, but some units actually used VC/NVA grey or light green uniforms when such uniforms gave them a tactical advantage. In garrison, most PRU members wore either civilian clothes or the standard PRU tiger-striped camouflage uniform. This wide variety

A more typical Provincial Reconnaissance Unit operation showing uniforms and equipment as worn by the Vietnamese and Americans. This was more characteristic than the VC or NVA uniforms shown before.

of uniforms made it difficult for both the enemy and friendly units to identify them. Therefore, it was essential that the U.S. PRU advisors coordinate closely with friendly units if the PRU were to operate in areas where U.S. and ARVN units were located. The Marine PRU advisors normally wore black pajamas or tiger-striped camouflage uniforms in the field and civilian clothes while in garrison. Some advisors even wore civilian clothes on PRU operations but this was rare.

Weapons consisted primarily of M-16 rifles, 45-caliber pistols, M-79 grenade launchers, and M-60 machine guns. However, many PRU units maintained extensive armories of captured weapons, and they often used these in operations against the VCI. The PRUs found it convenient to equip some of their men with Communist-made AK-47 rifles and RPG grenade launchers, so any VCI encountered during an operation in enemy territory would initially think they were fellow VC. This gave the PRUs a distinct tactical advantage in any engagement.[17]

This ploy of using enemy weapons became dangerous after late 1967 when the CIA began planting doctored AK-47 and other enemy ammunition in enemy stockpiles. These doctored rounds would explode when fired, causing serious, often fatal, wounds to those firing

11

them.[18] Still, despite this serious risk, many PRUs continued to use enemy weapons and ammunition after 1967 when they thought the risk was worth it. Other weapons that were employed by PRU members and their advisors were Browning 9-mm automatic pistols, 38-caliber Colt Cobra revolvers, Browning automatic rifles (BAR), M-2 carbines, Swedish K submachine guns, and British Bren guns. This wide assortment of weapons posed a logistical challenge to some PRU teams, but in most cases there were never any serious shortages of ammunition. Captured enemy ammunition was readily available, and the CIA supply system worked wonders in obtaining just about any ammunition required for operational use. Ammunition for the PRU was often stored in ConEx boxes within the CIA "embassy house" compounds or in the various PRU armories throughout the provinces so it could be rapidly issued.

For communications, the PRUs were equipped with the PRC-25 FM radio and its ancillary equipment. A few PRU units maintained some high frequency radios for long-range communications, but such radios were not standard issue, and most PRUs needed to establish temporary radio relay sites on mountaintops to support their long-range missions. This was especially true in the mountainous areas of I Corps. The PRUs were given their own frequencies for tactical communications. They were wary of the enemy intercepting their radio communications, so they seldom used their radios for the transmission of operational details while they were in garrison, choosing instead to use their radios sparingly and primarily during field operations. The PRUs had neither encrypted communications equipment nor code pads, so communications security was often nonexistent, ad hoc, or rudimentary. One of many valuable assets an American PRU advisor brought with him whenever he accompanied a PRU team to the field was the ability to encode communications; however, the use of encoding materials was not frequently employed during most PRU operations, even those that were accompanied by U.S. PRU advisors. Some PRUs did not use radios on their operations, preferring to maintain complete silence until the mission was completed.

PRU forces were equipped with ground transport in the form of commercial light trucks and motorcycles, which were purchased by the CIA. These trucks and motorcycles were typical of the trucks and motorcycles used by Vietnamese civilians, so their use did not arouse suspicion or draw unwanted attention to them when they were employed by the PRU. It also made repair of these transport assets easy since parts, automotive supplies, and repairs could be readily obtained locally. When major repairs were needed, PRU vehicles were taken to the CIA's automotive repair facility in Saigon.

Unfortunately, the trucks and motorcycles were never provided in the numbers needed by the PRU. Often, only two to three trucks were given to each province, thus they had to be shared by each district team or kept at province level for use as needed. Most PRU teams suffered because of the lack of organic transport. As a result, the PRUs also used public transportation, such as cyclos and buses, or privately owned motorcycles or bicycles to insert themselves into operational areas. Dressed in civilian clothes and posing as civilian travelers, they were able to blend in with the locals using these modes of transportation until they were near their operational area and ready to engage their targets.[19]

Although most PRU operations did not require U.S. military or ARVN transportation assets, the PRUs did avail themselves of such transport when it was provided to them, usually through the good offices of the Vietnamese province chief, a district U.S. military advisor, or the U.S. PRU advisor. For operations over long distances and in mountainous terrain, the PRUs would rely primarily on U.S. helicopters for insertion and extraction. Most U.S. PRU advisors felt the PRUs would have been even more effective had they possessed additional organic transportation assets, such as three-quarter-ton trucks and motorcycles, and a dedicated helicopter package in each military region. The U.S. PRU advisors stated that they often lost valuable time trying to obtain nonorganic transportation for deep or difficult PRU operations, and these delays often had an adverse impact on the success rate of such operations. Since most PRU targets were fleeting in nature, a timely response, often within 24 hours, was needed to achieve success. The lack of organic or rapidly available transportation assets often meant that the target was gone by the time the transportation had been arranged.

As stated earlier, the PRUs were under the operational control of the CIA. However, under an agreement between the GVN and the CIA, the Vietnamese province chiefs were given some control over how and when the PRUs could be used. In some instances, this dual-command relationship caused friction between the local CIA leadership in the province and the province chiefs. The relationship was certainly a violation of the unity of command principle. Theoretically, all PRU operations in a province required both the approval of the provincial officer in charge (POIC), who was the senior CIA officer in the province, and the province chief. In many provinces, the PRUs followed this arrangement, but in some provinces, the CIA disregarded it.

In the case of the author, he followed the dual command relationship procedures and encountered little problem with it in his province. He had few problems obtaining dual authorization for a mission, usually obtaining the approval of both his POIC and province chief in a matter of a few hours. He did this by having his Vietnamese PRU operations officer use a standard-form arrest order for each VCI suspect identified, then he would hand carry the arrest order to the province chief after the POIC had initialed his concurrence. In some cases, the author was also required to obtain the signature of the provincial judicial representative on the Provincial Intelligence Operations Coordination Committee to ensure that the arrest order was issued properly and with the necessary legal safeguards.[20]

Some PRU advisors simply obtained the per-

mission of the POIC and assumed the POIC would get the province chief's approval. As the program matured, the necessity to fully coordinate PRU arrest orders and operations with the province chiefs became institutionalized. One positive aspect of this dual approval system was the increased cooperation it generated between the Vietnamese and American agencies assigned counter-VCI duties. It also helped to break down suspicion among the Vietnamese Phoenix agencies that the CIA was acting alone and without consideration of the sovereignty of the Vietnamese government.

The PRU command and control authority on the Vietnamese side came down from the president through the minister of interior to the province chiefs and finally down to the district chiefs, but this was more administrative than operational since day-to-day operations of the PRUs were planned and executed under the direct supervision of the CIA. In a practical sense, the CIA POICs controlled the PRUs and used the American PRU advisors to ensure the PRU teams were properly employed on counter-VCI operations.

A great deal of authority and independence of action was given to the PRU advisors, often amounting to outright autonomy. Since many POICs were busy with their primary duties, not the least of which was the collection of political and strategic intelligence on the enemy's Central Office South Vietnam (COSVN) and the North Vietnamese government, they simply did not have the time to micromanage the PRU advisor. Also, many POICs lacked military experience or their military experience was dated. This meant that they did not feel they had the technical expertise to plan and control the types of operations the PRUs were conducting and preferred to leave the operational details to the initiative of the American PRU advisors.

Because the PRU advisors had a great deal of control over how and when their PRU teams were employed, the job required a level of maturity and sophistication not commonly found among the normal special operations soldier, sailor, or Marine. The American PRU advisors

13

were unanimous in their recommendation that the best men for assignment to this form of duty should be in the age range of 25 to 30 years old and should have obtained at least the equivalent rank of sergeant (E-5) for enlisted and first lieutenant (O-2) for officers. Ideally, they felt the enlisted advisors should be the equivalent of gunnery sergeants (E-7) and the officers should be captains (0-3). Command and control of PRU-type units required objectivity, maturity, and sound judgment—all traits that can only be developed with time and experience. The American PRU advisors were unanimous in their belief that immaturity and emotionalism were two of the most destructive and corrosive characteristics a PRU advisor could possess and, along with a lack of cultural sensitivity, the root causes of most serious problems.

The number of U.S. military PRU advisors was small; perhaps no more than 400 were assigned to the program from 1967 to 1971. Of that number, the author has been able to identify 51 Marines who served with PRUs as advisors. See the Appendix for a list of these Marine PRU advisors.

The experiences of the PRU advisors varied with their respective units and the provinces in which they served. As the Phoenix program matured and the PRU developed into a truly nationwide organization, the Marine PRU advisors helped mold and shape this development. The following firsthand accounts will give the reader an idea of how the advisory effort progressed from its inception until the last U.S. military advisors were removed.

Sergeant Paul C. Whitlock: One of the First and Best, 1966-1967

Sergeant Whitlock's outstanding performance in Quang Tri led the CIA to ask for more such fine men to assist the CIA's PRU advisory effort. His input is extremely valuable in explaining how he easily fit in and contributed positively to Agency paramilitary field programs.

Rudy Enders [21]

Paul C. Whitlock was a young staff sergeant serving as a reconnaissance team leader in the 3d Force Reconnaissance Company in October 1966 when he was called into the office of his commanding officer, Captain Kenneth Jordan, and told he was to report to work in Quang Tri City and "form a reconnaissance unit there" for special police operations. Staff Sergeant Whitlock asked Captain Jordan why he had been selected for this assignment, and Jordan simply replied, "because you are a Marine." Whitlock knew better than to ask any more questions, and besides, he trusted Jordan and knew there must be a good reason why he wanted him to go to Quang Tri City. Whitlock was one of the first Marines assigned to the PRU Program and he remained with the Quang Tri PRU from October 1966 until May 1967. The CIA officers who knew Whitlock spoke highly of him and stated that as one of the first Marines assigned to the PRU in I Corps, he set the standard for every Marine who followed.

When Whitlock reported to his CIA boss in Quang Tri, he found a recently organized PRU, one that had been staffed with former members of the Counter Terrorist Team (CTT) for Quang Tri. His unit consisted of 200 men, led by a very capable PRU chief and already conducting operations against the VCI. He immediately struck up a strong professional relationship with the PRU chief, and this relationship remained healthy throughout the eight months that Whitlock was the Quang Tri PRU advisor. Whitlock considered the PRU chief to be a strong leader who enjoyed the respect of his men and the Americans who worked with him.

Whitlock also had an excellent relationship with the province chief. He stated that he and the province chief "worked well together," noting that "he helped out when and where he could." It was evident from Whitlock's comments to the author that having both a capable and strong PRU chief and a reliable and cooperative province chief made his job easier and his work more effective than it would have been without these two key men assisting him. Whitlock also had high praise for his boss, the

14

POIC, Thomas D. Harlan. Harlan worked in what was labeled the Office of Civil Operations for Quang Tri Province. According to Whitlock, Harlan helped him whenever he needed help, provided him with many excellent operational leads, and backed him up "100 percent."

The Quang Tri PRU had two types of operations. They were based upon the geography of the province. "Deep" missions were those that were conducted in the western mountains of the province in such areas as the Bei Lon Valley, Khe Sanh, and the Quang Tri and Bei Lon rivers. These missions were assigned by the 3d Marine Amphibious Force (III MAF) headquarters and could best be described as long-range reconnaissance missions since their main purpose was to determine what the NVA units in those areas were doing. As such, they were not the classic counter-VCI mission normally assigned to a PRU. These operations were coordinated with III MAF by the POIC, Tom Harlan, and employed "handpicked teams" of PRU members. The teams were normally inserted and extracted by Marine helicopters. Prior to insertion on these "deep" missions, the PRU team, which normally consisted of five to seven men, was isolated and only briefed on the location of the mission just prior to departure. This was done to ensure operational security. Some of these "deep" missions required Whitlock to establish radio relay stations on prominent terrain features so the teams would have continuous FM radio contact with PRU headquarters.

The second type of mission the Quang Tri PRU conducted was the "coastal" mission. This entailed operating in the eastern section of the province in the populated coastal plain. These operations involved teams of 10 to 15 men. The means of insertion and extraction varied from Marine helicopters to commercial boats and other forms of transportation readily available. The focus of the "coastal" missions was the capture of VCI, not reconnaissance. As such, they were equipped, dressed, and armed for raid operations against known or suspected VCI targets.

The Quang Tri PRU dressed in tiger-striped camouflage uniforms, black pajamas, and NVA light green uniforms, depending on the conditions and the mission. The only civilian clothes they wore were the ubiquitous black pajamas worn by peasants in the countryside. The unit employed PRC-25 radios for communications, and they carried an assortment of weapons, which were issued depending on the mission. For instance, "deep" mission teams normally were armed with M-16 rifles, while "coastal" missions used M-1 and M-14 rifles and M-2 carbines.

Whitlock described his PRU as "very well trained." This was so because Whitlock made it so. Like most PRU advisors, he spent a lot of time in garrison training his troops. Most of his training "involved land navigation, radio procedures, reconnaissance techniques, weapons training and small unit tactics." He possessed well-developed organizational skills and was able to increase the strength of his unit from 200 to 300 men, all while maintaining a professional force, well trained and well equipped for their mission.

Whitlock identified the main strength of his PRU as "the ability to move around when and where others could not....They knew the terrain and the people." The one serious problem he had with his unit was the lack of reliability of some of the PRU members to carry out their mission properly. Specifically, he often could not be sure they went where they were instructed to go or carried out their mission as he wanted them to unless he went along on the mission. Later on, he developed a means for checking on their veracity when he did not accompany them on an operation. He did this by assigning a different insert and extraction location for each mission. By doing this, the PRU team had to travel from its insertion location through the area Whitlock wanted covered in order to reach its extraction location.

The best source of intelligence on the VCI in Quang Tri Province was the intelligence generated by the PRU using local people. The Quang Tri PRU members "had their own system for gathering intelligence," according to

Whitlock, and it proved to be accurate where most other sources were not. Whitlock would send his PRU members and their families out into their home villages to develop operational leads. "They were to pay attention to their surroundings and report back. . . . Once the PRU and their family members developed enough information on the local VCI, the PRU would launch an operation." Whitlock also identified prisoner interrogation by the PRU as a valuable source of exploitable intelligence.

Whitlock offered this advice for future Marines involved in a counterinsurgency like the one he fought in during the Vietnam War: "Find an in-country leader who you can trust and communicate with effectively. Also, if you can't speak the local language, find a good interpreter who will follow your instructions completely and will translate exactly what you have said without embellishment." [22]

CIA officer Rudy Enders, who was the chief of operations in I Corps when Whitlock was first assigned to the PRU, thought Whitlock possessed in abundance the qualities needed for a PRU advisor. He wrote:

There are many qualifications associated with being an effective PRU advisor. Let's take Whitlock as an example. First of all, he was an experienced, brave combat leader who could assess the capabilities and shortcomings of the men he advised. If necessary, he could train them in every aspect of small unit tactics starting with basic shooting, fire and maneuver, scouting and patrolling, map and compass, etc. . . . I understand he did this. Furthermore, he singled out his PRU commander, Do Bach, as a heroic, competent warrior. To gain PRU confidence, he accompanied Bach on dangerous missions proving he was willing to lay his life on the line while fighting alongside his men. This is what leadership is all about.

Secondly, Whitlock was mature. He was not some wide-eyed kid looking for adventure. Instead, he understood the seriousness of his position and behaved accordingly. I can't overstate the importance of this attribute. PRU advisors performed their jobs with

very little oversight and supervision. This requires a high degree of self-discipline and commitment common to most Marines.

Finally, Whitlock was aggressive. He sifted through mountains of intelligence reports to find the most promising. His PRUs didn't sit around in camp waiting for things to happen, they made things happen. They sought out the enemy, enough so that the North Vietnamese sent a special sapper unit to destroy the PRU camp. The point is, a single Marine, Whitlock, with CIA help, produced an effective and aggressive South Vietnamese counterinsurgency force of over 300 men. [23]

Staff Sergeant Whitlock was one of the first and best U.S. military PRU advisors and, as such, he became a model for the advisors that followed. His POIC, Thomas Harlan, summed up the contributions of Whitlock in a letter he wrote to the commanding general, 3d Marine Division, on 3 April 1967 thanking the general for sending such a highly trained and capable NCO to the PRU Program. Harlan wrote that Whitlock "displayed unique dedication, imagination, and knowledge of his job. . . . [T]he PRUs under his guidance have distinguished themselves in long range reconnaissance patrols and unconventional warfare operations. . . . [H]is methods are being adapted throughout I Corps with all Provincial Reconnaissance Units being patterned after the one in Quang Tri Province."

Whitlock retired from the Marine Corps as a gunnery sergeant in 1974 and then worked four years with a high school Junior ROTC program before embarking on a 20-year career as a project manager for a major commercial contracting firm.

Sergeant Ronald J. Lauzon: Hue City, 1967

Sergeant Ronald J. (Ron) Lauzon had 12 years of military experience—six with the Air Force and six with the Marines—when he was assigned to the PRU on 8 March 1967. His assignment took him to Hue City in Thua Thien Province, and he remained with the PRU in Hue City until he was reassigned to the Marine

Sergeant Ronald J. Lauzon on operations with the Thua Thein Provincial Reconnaissance Unit in 1967. Marine advisors wore utility, tiger-stripe, or even black "pajama" uniforms while in the field. Note the lack of distinguishing rank or other insignia.

Corps on 8 October 1967. He described the time he spent as a PRU advisor as "a great experience for an E-5/E-6 during the peak of the program," and one he considered the most rewarding of his Marine Corps career. He retired from the Marine Corps as a chief warrant officer (CWO-4). Lauzon provided the following selected comments in a paper he submitted to the author:

I relieved Sergeant Robert B. Bright III as the PRU advisor for Thua Thien Province. He had done an outstanding job of organizing, training, equipping, and establishing coordination for the unit. I inherited a PRU unit of 137 soldiers, but I paired it down to 117, and I lost seven killed in combat during the seven months I was their advisor.

I did not have much bush time with the unit; most of the 100 or so operations I sponsored were small-unit actions aimed at gaining or supporting intelligence requested by

the Regional Officer in Charge (ROIC) and, as such, participation on them was restricted to indigenous personnel. On most of our operations, a Caucasian would not have fit in, and the CIA was paranoid about having someone captured by the enemy who possessed internal knowledge of how the CIA operated.

I did go on major military operations which were requested by MACV, USMC, or ARVN units, but these operations were all ultimate disasters for the PRU since they were employed as regular ground forces, and they were not trained or equipped for such employment. Many times these large-scale missions were misrepresented to CORDS as missions appropriate for the PRU, but in every case they turned into standard military type operations against main force VC or NVA units.

I principally served out of Hue City and

17

stayed in the PRU compound, which was Madame Nhu's summer home.* This compound sat on the northwest corner of the Hue perimeter overlooking the Royal Tombs. My area of operations was the entire province with the exception of Hue City. The city was solely reserved for the CORDS intelligence section, which had a number of USMC counterintelligence personnel assigned to it. They worked out of the National Police Intelligence Center, and they relied heavily on the province's Police Special Branch (PSB), which gathered most of its intelligence from the province's interrogation center (PIC).

I did not live in an "embassy house," like many other PRU advisors. Instead, I lived in a leased house in southern Hue across from a large Roman Catholic cathedral close to the Phu Can Canal along Nguyen Hue Street. This house was where my replacement was killed and where Ray Lau spent a couple of days in a pigsty hiding from the VC during the Tet Offensive when the enemy controlled the city. I rotated where I slept almost nightly during my PRU tour, spending some nights at my house, some at the PRU barracks, some at Ray Lau's, some at the POIC's house, and some at other trusted locations. We were often on alert for an attack, and we kept arms and ammunition stored in our house in case we came under attack.

PRU operations varied from province to province based upon the enemy situation in each province and the priorities of the CIA and the province chiefs. In our case, the POIC and his assistant strictly wanted the PRU to generate intelligence and not lose any assets. There was no doubt in anyone's mind that assassinations were strictly forbidden. This was stressed by both Colonel Redel,[24] who briefed me in Saigon during my indoctrination, and by my training instructors at the CIA PRU training base at Vung Tau in III Corps. My PRU teams were strictly focused

on obtaining intelligence about the VCI in my province and ensuring this intelligence was put to good use by the various Vietnamese and American units in the province.

Since I had access to all the intelligence resources in I Corps, I could pick up the latest reports from the MACV compound, the Special Forces SOG Headquarters, the 3d Marine Division G-2, the 8th Radio Relay Unit (RRU), the Army Side Looking Radar and Infrared Assessments, and the PIC. I would read through these reports each night looking for any information about the latest movements of the National Liberation Front (NLF) committee members. This included the VC paymasters, recruiters, party organizers, armed propaganda teams, and assassination squads. Once I picked a couple of targets, I would go to the PRU compound early in the morning and brief the PRU Commander, Mr. Mau. We would agree on one or two missions and assign the missions to the platoon leader on duty, who would select the men, uniforms, and equipment for the missions. We had two 30-man rifle platoons; a 30-man weapons platoon equipped with 60mm mortars, RPGs, and crew-served machine guns; and a headquarters section, which included intelligence, logistics, armory, and first-aid personnel.

Once the teams were identified for the mission, they were put into isolation. The PRU intelligence section would brief them on the mission and any pertinent information they had on the target(s), the supply section would issue them their special equipment (cameras, binoculars, sensors, radios, etc.), and the armory would issue them their ammunition and special weapons (sniper rifles, claymore mines, satchel charges, pistols, etc.).

The majority of the 117 PRU I ultimately ended up with were holdovers from the previous Counter Terrorist Team (CTT) program in the province. We also had 13 active PRU intelligence agents in the field. We had very little turnover, and we were very selective in whom we chose to join our ranks. A few of our men were former VC, and some were for-

---

*Madame Nhu was the flamboyant wife of Ngo Dinh Nhu, the younger brother and chief advisor of Ngo Dinh Diem, who was president of South Vietnam until he and his brother were assassinated in 1963.

mer ARVN Rangers and Marines who had completed their military service but wanted to join the PRU in their home province. All of my PRU were local people, and they came from all eight districts, which meant they had firsthand knowledge of the terrain and people where they were operating. Most had served in the military, either VC or ARVN, and they had been trained at the PRU training center in Vung Tau and at the Reconnaissance Indoctrination Program (RIP) school at the 1st Marine Division at Da Nang. They were, in my opinion, well trained and highly experienced soldiers. I liked the PRU I worked with and had complete confidence in the team leaders and the PRU Commander, Mr. Mau.

All operations in the province were centrally planned and controlled out of the PRU compound in Hue City. To my knowledge, we did not have active DIOCCs in the eight districts in our province and, if we did, I had no contact with them. To be honest, I only trusted our own intelligence system, which was operated by the RD/PRU/CG/CI intelligence center in Hue City.

The operational PRU teams were usually small, four or five men, with one of the men familiar with the area of operations and the people living there. They would dress either in civilian clothes or VC uniforms and be equipped with AK-47 rifles, French pistols, M-1 carbines, and hand grenades. They would be inserted late in the day but before curfew at a neutral point as close to the target area as possible, either by public transportation or taxicab. Sometimes they went by bicycle or used U.S. Navy swift boats for insertion. We often used U.S. Marine Combined Action Platoon (CAP) compounds in the countryside to launch operations, and we considered these CAP areas ideal for the insertion of our teams since they could provide coordination with higher headquarters in the 3d Marine Division and a safe haven once an operation was completed.

After a team was inserted, I went to the MACV compound and reported the opera-

tional plan. I reported the operation after insertion because I did not want any enemy agents in the MACV compound to reveal the operation to the NLF.

While I was a PRU advisor, I read literally hundreds of intelligence reports from the U.S. and South Vietnamese military, and not a single one was either timely or totally accurate. The military intelligence reports were written with specific times and dates with specific map coordinates and numbers, but I found out from dozens of interrogations that the VCI did not read or use map coordinates—they just used place names such as Cam Lo Bridge or Phouc Ly Village—and they measured time by "after a specific event, soon, pretty soon, or now." The unit descriptions used in the military reports meant nothing to me since a "VC squad" could number between 1 and 50 men and a "VC company" could number between a dozen and several hundred men.

We mounted over 100 operations during my tour with the PRU, and 11 of these were

Sergeant Lauzon in garrison with a member of the Thua Thein Provincial Reconnaissance Unit in 1967. In these circumstances, civilian clothes were usally worn.

Photo courtesy of CWO-4 Ronald J. Lauzon

successful in capturing or killing VCI. There were only two sources for these 11 successful missions: the PRU's organic intelligence system and Ray Lau's RD Census Grievance element, which gathered information from the RD team's travels in the province. We never got any operational leads that resulted in a successful operation from any other source, including the PIC and the PSB.

These successful missions were either an ambush or a raid on a specific house or area that we knew had VCI in it. When a mission was completed, which normally lasted only 24 hours, the PRU team would call in by telephone, and they would be picked up by a PRU vehicle or an RD vehicle at the nearest highway. Captured prisoners were brought back to the PRU compound and interrogated by Mr. Mau and his PRU intelligence team. After we had them for 24 hours, we were supposed to turn them over to the PIC and the military interrogation center with the USMC CI representative, but after a visit to these facilities, I never turned any more prisoners over to them. If the prisoners were high value (Category A or B), we shipped them to Da Nang City for interrogation by the CIA, but if they were low-level cadre, such as a nurse or paymaster, we often simply interrogated them and sent them home, or in the case of two individuals, we allowed them to join the PRU.

The only serious trouble we had was the result of conflicts between U.S. and Vietnamese officials concerning who controlled the PRU. CORDS paid the bills and ran the operation, but the province chief believed the PRU was his to use as he saw fit. This conflict often resulted in the misuse of the PRU and placed me in the middle of these bureaucratic and political battles. Cooperation and coordination were sometimes a problem in my province because of this ambiguous command relationship.

My boss was the CIA's POIC. I had two bosses during my tour, one of whom left shortly after I was assigned. The second POIC was a "CIA paramilitary type" who prohib-

ited me from participating in any PRU operations. He preferred to have only Vietnamese participate in PRU operations. His rationale for this was his conviction that "native ingenuity" would find innovative ways for the PRU to accomplish their missions, and "since it was going to be a long war, they needed assets with experience operating on their own." My POIC was supportive and gave me a great deal of latitude in how I should do my job. I left the PRU just before the 1968 Tet Offensive, and my POIC was in Da Nang City when the VC/NVA struck. He was in the process of turning his job over to his replacement, who had just settled into his quarters in Hue City. The new POIC was captured by the NVA when they invaded Hue City. He spent the rest of the war as a POW.

My replacement as PRU advisor, Sergeant Howard Vaughn, reported for duty a few weeks after I left and was killed defending the embassy house during the 1968 Tet Offensive.[25]

Staff Sergeant Wayne W. Thompson: Leadership Challenges and Spies, 1967–68

Staff Sergeant Wayne Thompson was a reconnaissance team leader with the 1st Force Reconnaissance Company in July 1967 when he was told by his commanding officer, Captain King Dixon, that he was to be reassigned to "a classified special project" that needed someone with his skills. A few days later, he was driven to a large villa in Da Nang and introduced to a civilian who told him he was going to work with a program run by the CIA in Quang Tin Province. He was briefed on the PRU Program and its mission, but he received no training for his new job. After in-processing, he reported to his new job in Quang Tin. He lived in the embassy house in Tam Ky, the provincial capital, with three other Americans who were also assigned to the CIA, men he knew as "Richard," an Army sergeant major; "Harry"; and "Jim." Together, the four men ran the CIA operations for Quang Tin Province.

Thompson was a gifted and highly experienced

Marine staff noncommissioned officer. He had extensive experience with reconnaissance operations having served in both the 2d and 1st Force Reconnaissance Companies, including several long-range reconnaissance patrols in combat in Vietnam. He possessed the maturity and the skills needed to succeed in his new demanding job. As it would turn out, he would need those skills and then some.

Thompson's first major problem was a very serious one. His PRU Chief, a Nung and not a native Vietnamese, was "incompetent and lazy" and considered "a thief" by everyone, according to Thompson. His PRU of approximately 50 men did not venture outside of the compound, which was located on the perimeter of the provincial compound. His PRU chief contended that he was not allowed to leave the compound because the province chief, an ARVN lieutenant colonel, did not want to weaken the provincial compound's security.

Thompson knew that he would never be able to accomplish his mission of defeating the VCI if this situation persisted. He fired the PRU chief 10 days after his arrival in Quang Tin, then he went to the province chief to work out the security arrangement that was preventing his PRU teams from conducting their proper mission. The province chief told him that the PRUs were the only fighters he could really rely on to protect the provincial compound and that he could not allow them to relinquish this essential security mission. Thompson worked out a deal with the province chief. In return for using 50 men to guard the provincial compound's perimeter, he promised to increase the size of the PRU until he had enough additional men to conduct counter-VCI missions. With the CIA's permission, he began recruiting the additional men until he had 145 to 155 men on the PRU roles. Some of his best new recruits were VC prisoners held in the provincial prison who were carefully vetted before they were allowed to join the ranks of the PRU.

Next, Thompson addressed the issue of who would be the replacement for the PRU chief he had just fired. The province chief recommended an elderly gentleman who was a political ally of the province chief but clearly a man who lacked the military or leadership skills needed to command a PRU. Thompson got around this sensitive problem by convincing the province chief that he would put the elderly gentleman recommended by the province chief in charge of the PRU security force of 50 men guarding the provincial compound and put a more competent and aggressive young former ARVN soldier in charge of the counter-VCI mission, appointing him as the "Deputy PRU Chief for Operations." The province chief found this solution perfectly suitable since he did not lose face by having his choice for PRU chief rejected, he would have someone he trusted in charge of local security around the provincial compound, and Thompson would have the combat leader he needed to root out the VCI. Using tact, good judgment, and an innovative approach, Thompson was able to overcome daunting problems early in his assignment with the Quang Tin PRU and to win the respect, cooperation, and support of the province chief at the same time.

During his eight months with the Quang Tin PRU, Thompson's PRU racked up a commendable record by killing or capturing more than 300 VC, NVA, and VCI while losing only nine PRU killed in action. Much of this success was due to the intelligence system that Thompson helped to develop for the PRU. He knew that he could not rely on external sources for intelligence on the VCI, although he did occasionally receive actionable intelligence from the Census Grievance and Special Branch advisors who lived with him in the embassy house. He decided that he had to form his own intelligence organization for Quang Tin Province if he wanted his PRU to be truly effective. He did this by recruiting six to ten agents distributed geographically throughout the areas either controlled or contested by the enemy. His agents were nominally paid for their information but only received payments for information that was proven to be true or resulted in the capture of VCI.

Late in his tour with the PRU, Thompson's

intelligence system generated accurate intelligence concerning a high-ranking VCI living in a house in a contested area west of Tam Ky. This information resulted in a combined force of 50 PRU soldiers and a battalion of the U.S. 1st Cavalry Division making a mechanized assault into the village where the VCI cadre was hiding. This operation not only bagged the VCI target but also resulted in the defeat of an NVA battalion defending the village.

Thompson left the Quang Tin PRU in March 1968, but he returned to Vietnam in 1969, serving again with the 1st Force Reconnaissance Company in Quang Nam Province. He was seriously injured during an emergency helicopter extraction using a STABO (Short Tactical Airborne Operation) rig, which resulted in his hospitalization for a year and eventual medical discharge from the Marine Corps in 1970. He left the Corps with the rank of gunnery sergeant.[26]

First Lieutenant Joel R. Gardner: A Marine in II Corps, 1967-68

First Lieutenant Joel R. Gardner was bored with his job of teaching French to officers enrolled in the Marine Corps' Command and Staff College at Quantico, Virginia. So one morning in February 1967 when he saw a message posted on the school's bulletin board that sought volunteers for a special assignment, he saw a chance to escape from that billet. The message was rather cryptic. It simply solicited "volunteers with Vietnam experience for detached duty." Although the message contained no additional details, Lieutenant Gardner suspected this duty had something to do with the Central Intelligence Agency, and this appealed to his sense of adventure and his desire to return to where the action was—in Vietnam.

Gardner came from a distinguished military family. He was the son of a retired U.S. Navy admiral, and he had followed in his father's footsteps by graduating from the U.S. Naval Academy in the class of 1963. After the Basic School, he had served as a platoon commander in A/1/4 before volunteering for duty as a platoon commander with Company B, 3d Recon-

naissance Battalion. While with 3d Recon Battalion, he had made the initial landings at Chu Lai and had distinguished himself in combat, earning three Bronze Stars and two Purple Hearts before his tour ended in March 1966.

With his Vietnam experience and his desire to return to the fight, Gardner willingly volunteered for the "detached duty" without having any more knowledge of what was expected of him. He only knew that if he was accepted for this new and potentially exciting work, he would no longer have to teach French. He felt confident that any new assignment would be more exciting than his present one. He was not disappointed.

Lieutenant Gardner drove to Headquarters Marine Corps in the Navy Annex in Arlington, Virginia, to formally apply for the new job. He was interviewed Colonel Noble Beck in the personnel department and, evidently, the interview went well because one week later, Gardner received orders "to such place in Washington, D.C., as would be designated in separate correspondence." Thus began a two-year sojourn with the Central Intelligence Agency on independent orders.

What follows is the tale of Lieutenant Gardner's experience in his own words as one of only a very few Marines assigned to duty as a PRU advisor in the II Corps of Vietnam:

We started our training/orientation in Washington, D.C., with a group of over 50 military officers, mostly U.S. Army officers and only seven Marine officers. The CIA was in a hurry for us to get to Vietnam since many of their career case officers were up for reassignment from Vietnam to jobs for which they were more appropriately trained; that is, working against the Soviet Union and its satellites. These CIA career officers were needed for operations against the main enemy, not for operations in some "side show" like Vietnam. This meant we would receive a shortened case-officer training program so we could rapidly replace them.

After an initial briefing and psychological and "lifestyle" testing, we began our formal training program. Part of the training was at a "remote or southern training facility" where we were introduced to the arcane tradecraft of intelligence. I would return later in my Marine Corps career in 1980 to this CIA training facility for additional training prior to my assignment as a naval attaché in Paris. We also went through a comprehensive area and language training course at the State Department's Foreign Service Institute Vietnam Training Center in Rosslyn, Virginia, where we achieved a 3/3 language proficiency rating upon graduation. At the completion of our training, which took approximately five months, we were given our official passports and other credentials identifying us as "USAID Rural Development Officers." I later told people that I was actually an agricultural expert on grasshoppers, but they seemed incredulous since I carried a Swedish K submachine gun all the time! I assured them that the Swedish K was needed because there were a lot of grasshoppers that needed to be exterminated, and we classified these grasshoppers as "Vermin, Communist Infestators," or VCI.

After relocating my wife and two children in Bangkok, Thailand, where they would stay until my 18-month tour of duty in Vietnam with the CIA ended, I flew to Saigon, arriving there in August 1967. After checking into the Duc Hotel, I went to the U.S. Embassy for a briefing on the situation in Vietnam and what my future duties might entail. I also checked in with USAID since they provided my cover and they handled my pay. My military records were maintained by the CSD/MACV unit at Tan Son Nhut Airport. This dual administrative arrangement resulted in receiving active-duty time for my military career while receiving civilian pay. It was all very confusing, but with three "masters" in charge of me (CIA, USAID, and DoD), I thought I would be able to fool all of them most of the time. Like most CIA personnel, my home while in Saigon was the Duc Hotel. It was my temporary abode during my initial orientation in Saigon and during subsequent visits to the capital city.

At the U.S. Embassy, I met Marine Colonel William Redel, who handled all PRU matters. He informed me that despite the Commandant's request to have all Marines assigned to I Corps, he was going to assign me to the coastal city of Nha Trang in Khanh Hoa province in II Corps. His rationale for this assignment was my recent combat experience with 3d Recon Battalion, which he felt would best benefit the program if applied in Khanh Hoa province working with the PRU there.

Nha Trang is the largest city in II Corps. I flew up to my new assignment aboard an Air America plane and reported to my new boss, Ernie Sparks, who was the ROIC for II Corps. Ernie's initial briefing to me was short and sweet since he was a man of few words, but his guidance was specific, and he made me feel welcome and appreciated at our first session together.

Being close to the ROIC HQ was both a problem and a blessing. The ROIC staff officers were always looking over my shoulder. However, having the regional supply facility and access to Air America helicopters and daily Volpar flights more than compensated for this inconvenient meddling. There was also the problem of visitors who came to the ROIC HQ for briefings, like Daniel Ellsberg, who managed to stay with us for three days! I showed him our "A" hamlets where we had RD cadre teams but kept him well away from the PRU and their operations. These visitors and the time it took to brief them often took me away from my "real work."

My time in Nha Trang started out with my being placed in charge of the province's 110-man PRU. The unit seemed well equipped and, supposedly, fully trained at the Vung Tau training facility operated by the CIA. However, I quickly found out that my PRU chief considered me a useless adjunct to his life. He would do the traditional Vietnamese thing of listening to my questions and giving me the answers he thought I wanted to hear, not what I needed to hear. He was distant, hard to find at times, and not prone to keep me informed. He was resentful when I said

I would be present at payday and I wanted to see everyone on the roles who was receiving pay. Needless to say, we did not get off to a good start.

When I arrived in Nha Trang, two other military officers arrived with me. They were both U.S. Army officers. We were to replace two CIA officers who were extremely anxious to leave, so our turnover briefing with them was rather short, and they were gone before we knew it. During this turnover, we were acutely aware of the difference between the CIA officers and us. It was pretty obvious that they did not think we were in the same league as they were.

One of these departing CIA officers had been in charge of the PRU, the CG, and the RD cadre programs. The other was responsible for the Police Special Branch and the PIC. We found that there were 25 59-man RD teams in the province and about 30 CG personnel conducting census surveys. One of us, an Army captain, took over the RD Program, and my other colleague, an Army major, took over the PSB and the PIC. I was given the PRU and Census Grievance Programs. Unfortunately, around Thanksgiving 1967, they were seriously wounded by a claymore mine and had to be evacuated from the country. For a time, I was the only man at the gate until an additional CIA officer, a Korean-American named Han Lee, came in and took the PSB and PIC off my hands. Still, trying to manage the PRU and RD Programs at the same time was a very heavy burden to bear, and I found it difficult to manage both large programs effectively. Fortunately, an Army Special Forces NCO, Staff Sergeant Joe Garza, joined us later, and he was placed in charge of the PRU under my immediate supervision.

After taking over the PRU, I tried to determine how they obtained intelligence for PRU operations. I was told that some operations were the result of information obtained from the RD cadre who reported on various people in certain families that were suspected of Communist sympathies. When they reported that these people were "out of town" for un-

known reasons, it often meant they were probably with the VC.

We also got information from the RD cadre on VCI tax collectors and armed propaganda teams, but I also knew the results of most of our PRU operations were pitiful. Staff Sergeant Garza and I at first thought we might have a "mole" in the unit giving away our operational plans to the enemy. We decided that we needed to find this mole as quickly as possible, so we devised a plan to give the entire PRU a polygraph examination in less than 24 hours. One night we secured the PRU armory and transferred all the weapons to the region's storage hanger at the Nha Trang airfield, and then the next day we had a polygraph team fly in from Saigon to administer the tests. The PRU members were apprehensive about taking a polygraph until we explained that they would not be hurt—unless they lied, and then they would be electrocuted!

The polygraph tests told us that we had not been infiltrated by a "mole," but the PRU chief and about half the PRU members were in collusion to fake operations. This entailed simply taking a team out on an "operation" to the edge of town, hiding for a few days, and then returning to base empty-handed. Needless to say, I fired the PRU chief and half the PRU immediately and began the process of finding honest replacements.

I found a new PRU chief who was highly recommended by the province chief and the province intelligence chief, which gave him both access to, and support from, these two important political leaders in the province. Staff Sergeant Garza and I got along very well with the new PRU chief, and with his help, we began recruiting local men for the PRU and sending them to the PRU training facility at Vung Tau. By Christmas 1967, we were back to full strength and conducting "real" operations against the VCI.

We concentrated our efforts against the VCI tax collectors since we knew that if we cut off the source of funds for the VC, we would seriously hurt the VC's ability to fi-

nance both their combat operations and political activities. Armed propaganda teams were also high on our list of targets, but as the term "armed' indicates, we often had more serious engagements with these VCI than with tax collectors. These two groups, the tax collectors and the armed propaganda teams, were the most visible to the local villagers, and their neutralization had the greatest impact on the villagers' perception of the efficiency of the PRU.

When I served in I Corps with a reconnaissance battalion, I had seen how special troops, like recon Marines, were inappropriately employed in operations they were neither trained nor equipped for, such as flank security for infantry sweeps, command post security, and assaults against fortified hamlets and villages. Using lightly armed, specially trained troops for missions they are not trained or equipped for is a foolish waste of valuable assets. The PRU teams were never meant to be used as infantry, but many U.S. and Vietnamese commanders did not understand the mission or capabilities of the PRU and, as a result, they often tried to use them on missions they were not suited for, often with disastrous results.

My PRU had an incredible inventory of weapons and equipment in its armory. The basic weapon for a PRU soldier was the Swedish K submachine gun, a heavy, rugged, and very reliable individual weapon. We also had sniper rifles (M-1s and Springfield 03s), carbines, LAWs, M-60 machine guns, silenced 22 caliber rifles, some British weapons, and enemy AK-47s for "black" operations.

The PRU was a direct support asset controlled completely at the provincial level. We did not have functioning DIOCCs in our province while I was there; that came much later on in the war. Since most of our province was covered in mountainous jungle and sparsely populated outside of a few areas, it made much more sense to use the PRU as a provincial level asset than to have it dispersed throughout the province. Nha Trang City and Ninh Hoa District north of

the city, along the lines of communication connecting the coastal plain with the highland cities of Dalat and Ben Me Thout, were where the population—and the VCI—were concentrated, and these areas were the focus of PRU operations.

I did not get along well with the U.S. province senior advisor, a U.S. Army lieutenant colonel, because he had some weird idea that I worked for him and thought I should keep him informed about what I was doing. I did, however, get along well with the district senior advisor in Ninh Hoa District, an Army major, who was very forward-looking and supportive of our capabilities.

As is so often in combat, great plans are driven by personalities, and this can make the difference between success and failure. An example of this involved an operation generated by cooperation between this supportive U.S. district advisor and our PRU. One day, he briefed me about a VCI tax team that was brazenly stopping traffic on the road between Ban Me Thout and Ninh Hoa on the coast. We met with the advisor's Vietnamese counterparts, and they briefed us on the modus operandi of this tax team. It seems the tax team would establish roadblocks at several points along the road to collect taxes from passing vehicles, and they tended to use some of these roadblocks regularly. They did not establish these roadblocks for long, just long enough to stop enough vehicles so they could meet their tax quotas for that day and then disappear back into the thick jungle.

Working with the U.S. advisor and the Vietnamese military, we worked on a plan to neutralize this VCI tax team. Staff Sergeant Garza, the PRU chief, and 15 PRU team members would be used to target one of the frequently used locations by the tax team. I hired a covered, civilian truck to transport this team to its ambush site, and then I joined up with the advisory team to the Korean Capitol Division near Ninh Hoa to set up a radio relay site five miles away. This was the first operation I allowed Staff Sergeant Garza to go on, and I did not want to *lose this valuable advisor. I gave him his own PRC-25 for communications. I also arranged for pre-planned artillery concentrations and a reaction force made up of a Vietnamese Ranger Company in case they were needed by the ambush team. As a rule, the Khanh Hoa PRU operated close to the densely populated areas of the province near the coast so this operation constituted a "deep" operation for us.*

The PRU ambush team set up on a hillside overlooking one of the favorite spots on the road that the VCI tax team used. Around noon on the second day, the PRU team observed the enemy tax team set up a collection point on the road 300 meters away. The PRU chief told the team to do nothing, only observe. He told Staff Sergeant Garza to wait until tomorrow when the tax team would return and the team would be in a better position to attack it. Staff Sergeant Garza explained to me the strict discipline of the PRU members as they remained motionless in their observation position for the next 24 hours, not even moving to make a head call. The next day, the VCI tax team returned to the road and set up their collection point directly under the PRU team's location. The PRU opened fire and killed the entire tax team. I do not think a U.S. unit would have waited 24 hours to initiate an ambush— Americans like instant gratification—but one cannot argue with the results.

Most of our operations were on a small scale, generally ambushes or interdictions based upon low-level intelligence and set up for specific targets moving into or between hamlets which had minimal or no GVN security forces (PF or RD cadre) in them. Generally, these targets were developed from leads generated at the local level and fed back through the Census Grievance representatives or RD Cadre teams working in the hamlets and villages. We also received leads from informants working for the Vietnamese military S-2s. I do not remember ever generating a plan or an operation from intelligence from a higher echelon, but the Vietnamese did this on occasion, as it should be.

I do not think it is accurate to say that the Americans were in command of the PRU in my province while I was there. We provided support: logistical, financial, and training. I ran interference for the PRU when people tried to misuse them or tried to take them over from us, but I considered the PRU to be under the command of the PRU chief and his team leaders, not me. They were, however, definitely under my operational control. I passed on intelligence gained by the PRU to the American side, primarily to First Field Force Vietnam Headquarters, the U.S. Air Force, and the Special Forces Headquarters at the Nha Trang air base.

We had one extraordinary operation in early January 1968. We received reports from either a CG or RD cadre that a person in one of the hamlets outside the city was providing food and other logistical support to an unknown enemy unit. Our suspect was a female who would carry "parcels" out of the hamlet almost daily and return empty-handed. We set up a series of surveillance operations over a period of several days, each one picking up where the previous one lost sight of her on her travels. They had her pretty well triangulated in an area of deep brush, scraggy trees, and rocky outcroppings. We wanted to use a PRU team to go into the area, but it was part of the Korean Logistical Command's TAOR, so we held off on the operation until we had their permission. Finally after some negotiating, we met with all the key players at the Korean Field Force HQ in Nha Trang and worked out the necessary coordination to make our operation possible.

Our operation was delayed a day because a Korean unit was in the area. That unit reported the area as empty and that our operation there would be a waste of our time. We went anyway, and in less than three hours, we found an occupied cave. The two occupants of the cave were killed in a short firefight, but the body count was not important. Inside the cave, we found records for the Nha Trang City Party Committee. It was a real intelligence bonanza and included a complete organizational chart for the party, 110 names of party members (AKA's to be sure), and other valuable documents. After Tet, which was only a few weeks after the operation, we captured enough prisoners so the Vietnamese could begin to put real names against the AKA's on the captured muster rolls. As a result, we were able to roll up almost the entire city party committee and deal a blow to the VCI that would set them back years.

This type of operation was the kind the PRU were designed for, and it demonstrates that one single piece of accurate intelligence provided by a local source, and properly exploited by a well-trained special police unit, can cause an entire insurgency infrastructure in a major city to be neutralized.

After my CIA assignment, I was assigned to the FSI Vietnam Training Center to train district and province senior advisors (civilian and military). I made regular trips back to South Vietnam during the period 1969-72 and would eventually visit nearly every district and province where we had advisory teams. During this time, I witnessed the maturation of the DIOCCs and the Phung Hoang Program and saw how Phung Hoang had become very effective in nearly all areas, inflicting serious losses on the VCI. Ho Chi Minh was quoted as saying that he was far more worried about our success against the VCI than against his regular forces. [27]

Lieutenant Colonel Terence M. Allen: The Perspective from Saigon, 1968-1970

When then-Lieutenant Colonel Terence M. (Terry) Allen reported for duty with the PRU as the chief advisor for military operations to the PRU commander in 1968, he brought with him a high degree of professional expertise and experience in special warfare. As the senior U.S. military advisor to the PRU in Saigon, he reported directly to the CIA's Tucker Gouglemann. Along with his able executive officer, Marine Major Kenneth D. Hyslop, they made up a formidable senior-level advisory team that

managed the U.S. side of the PRU Program during its most effective years from 1968 until 1970.

Prior to his assignment to the Combined Studies Division of MACV as the chief PRU advisor, Colonel Allen had been both the executive officer and commanding officer of the 3d Reconnaissance Battalion and the inspector and instructor for the 5th Force Reconnaissance Company. This experience gave him extensive firsthand knowledge about, and training in, the conduct of missions similar to those the PRU would routinely perform. His combat experience in Korea and his participation in operations in Lebanon in 1958 gave him a keen insight into unconventional warfare as well as a deep appreciation for the constraints often imposed on U.S. forces by geopolitical considerations. In short, he was an ideal choice for the military-political advisory role in which he found himself.

Living in an apartment in Saigon and working out of the PRU headquarters in Saigon, Allen ranged across the length and breadth of South Vietnam planning, organizing, and conducting various missions for the PRU. Not adverse to danger, he routinely accompanied PRU teams on missions in the provinces, including several parachute missions. He was also responsible for maintaining and analyzing the monthly reports that came into PRU headquarters from the U.S. advisors in the 44 provinces of South Vietnam and conducting inspections of the PRU teams operating throughout the country. As such, he had a unique perspective on the strengths and weaknesses of the PRU Program and its overall effectiveness in fighting the VCI. His near-daily interface with Nguyen Van Lang, the national commander of the PRU, allowed him to influence as well as assist the South Vietnamese PRU leadership in a way that no other American could.

Colonel Allen reinforced the widely held belief of most U.S. Marine PRU advisors that each PRU was unique based upon such factors as the province in which it was deployed, the ethnic and religious composition of the teams, the family and social connections, the military experience, the leadership, and the relationship with the CIA POICs and the South Vietnamese province chiefs. He also pointed out that geography often played a role in how the PRUs were employed and how their missions changed over time as the war progressed. For instance, he said that in the mountainous areas of South Vietnam where VCI were scarce, the PRUs often focused on collecting tactical intelligence rather than counter-VCI operations. In the coastal plains and the Mekong Delta where the population was dense, the PRUs were used in a wider array of missions depending on the level of pacification in their province.

As the pacification programs associated with Phoenix began to succeed after the 1968 Tet Offensive, and more and more hamlets were freed from VC control, the mission of the PRU evolved away from tactical intelligence and quasi-military operations to strictly counter-VCI, police-type operations. Colonel Allen also said that PRU teams even conducted several classified operations into the border areas of Cambodia against VCI known to be hiding there. These operations, because of their sensitivity, were planned and executed by the PRU directorate in Saigon.

In several interviews with the author, Colonel Allen mentioned two serious impediments to the PRU Program in particular and the Phoenix program in general. The first was the "obstruction and lack of cooperation by the U.S. State Department" when it came to PRU missions. He stated that he found the attitude of the State Department difficult to comprehend at times since their officials seemed to hold "the belief that as long as they were in control of events, the ambassador was second only to the President of the United States," an attitude that caused them to impose "controls on PRU employment that were both unnecessary and counterproductive." Many times the State Department representatives in South Vietnam dictated to Allen where Phoenix operations should be conducted, forcing him often to agree to these demands in principle but then to disregard them in practice. This lack of U.S. State Department cooperation and understanding for the PRU mission was a constant source of frustration for Allen as he worked diligently to coordinate PRU operations with other U.S. and South Vietnamese agencies.

While the State Department caused Colonel Allen the most concern, he also had difficulties with South Vietnamese province chiefs who misunderstood the proper role of the PRU or sought to use their local PRU for missions not related to the elimination of the VCI. He spent a considerable amount of time traveling around South Vietnam talking to province chiefs about this tendency to misuse the PRUs. His own MACV and Pacific Command intelligence analysts were also a problem at times since despite incontrovertible evidence, in the form of captured NVA or VC prisoners and enemy documents, they refused to believe the intelligence reports generated by the PRUs.

The second concern Colonel Allen had was the problems caused by what he described as inaccurate and false reporting by civilian journalists assigned to the Vietnam War. Allen's cover assignment was that of MACV deputy for public information. Although his title had nothing to do with his real job, it did give him access to considerable information on the press corps in South Vietnam. He soon found out that of the 565 reporters working in South Vietnam, few had either the background or the expertise to cover the kind of war being fought in South Vietnam, and many were openly sympathetic to the enemy cause. He also found that the North Vietnamese Intelligence Service, the Cuc Nghien Cuu, had thoroughly infiltrated the foreign press offices and were receiving classified information regularly from naïve and careless foreign reporters.

In addition to this classified information being used by the enemy to thwart the pacification effort, it was also being used by the enemy's agents within the foreign press corps to spread disinformation about Phoenix and other programs that were proving to be successful in hurting the enemy. So much inaccurate information about the PRU and the Special Operations Group (SOG) was being reported in the U.S. and foreign press in 1968 that Allen found it necessary to go the South Vietnamese minister for indigenous people, Paul Nur, and secure a promise from him to no longer refer to the Phoenix program or the PRU in any South Vietnamese press releases and to use the Vietnamese title of Phung Hoang instead. Allen considered the false and inaccurate reporting by journalists in the Saigon press corps to be far more damaging than anything the enemy did to hurt the PRU because these stories caused both the Lyndon B. Johnson and Richard M. Nixon administrations to overreact and impose restrictions on the PRU and their advisors that only served to help the enemy.

The author asked Colonel Allen several times about the claim that the PRUs engaged in assassinations and deliberately killed innocent civilians. He was adamant that the PRUs never received orders to assassinate anyone while he was the senior U.S. advisor to the PRU Program, and he knew of no instances prior to his assignment where such an order had been issued. He stated, just as the U.S. Marine advisors interviewed for this book did, that the PRU were given mission-type orders that directed them to conduct reconnaissance and surveillance operations, night ambushes, and raids on known or suspected VCI targets. He never issued an order to assassinate a VCI, only to capture one. As he stated, "the whole purpose of our operations was to capture VCI so we could interrogate them and benefit from the intelligence they provided. We did not benefit from killing a VCI since a dead VCI was of no intelligence value."[28]

Death at the Embassy House, Tet 1968

The PRU advisors' job was a very dangerous one. They lived with their CIA colleagues in villas that were often vulnerable to enemy attack, and in many instances they were the only Americans accompanying the PRU teams when they went on operations in areas controlled by the VC or NVA. The enemy feared the PRU and considered them and their advisors prime targets for elimination. The following account, written by Raymond R. Lau, who was a U.S. Marine captain assigned as a Rural Development advisor in Hue City at the time of the 1968 Tet Offensive, clearly illustrates how dangerous living in an embassy house could be. In his account, he tells the story of the death of Sergeant Howard G. Vaughn, the PRU advisor for Thua Thien Province.

Lau's commentary begins on the day before the Tet Offensive was launched, shortly after he had returned to Vietnam from extension leave. He had volunteered to spend an additional six months in Vietnam over his initial 13-month tour so he could continue to work with the Rural Development Program. His account is taken from an outline of events he wrote on 7 February 1968, the day he ended his harrowing seven days behind enemy lines.

After the short half-hour flight from Da Nang air base aboard an Air America flight, we landed at the small dirt airfield located in the northwest corner of the Citadel and I was met there by Jim Harris, a young former Special Forces, now with the embassy. We had become good friends in the short time we had known each other. We rode back into town in the jeep chatting about what happened during the past month, and we stopped at the Embassy Provincial Headquarters before going to the house where we were both staying. At the American compound, I met Tom Gompertz, a young FSO (Foreign Service Officer) assigned to Hue. He was the quintessential all-American boy, clean cut, good looking, with a ready smile that seemed to say that he was in on some joke. I'd known Tom since coming to Hue. We played soccer against the Nung guards and talked together often. Tom welcomed me back and said something about getting together soon, now that I was back. That was the last time I saw Tom until I identified his body some 10 days later. I visited his gravesite in 2002, finally "getting together" 35 years later.

That night after dinner, Jim and I chatted in the living room of our house while we

The Embassy House in Hue City after the Tet 1968 attack. At right is the Military Region 1 regional offi-cer-in-charge (ROIC), Mr. Harry Mustakos.

loaded the magazines of the Swedish K sub-machine guns that we had just gotten. Jim had gotten them that day and had grabbed one for me. It was like a new toy. We admired the weapons because of their simple unclut-tered design, the green metal body with its folding stock, its wooden pistol grip, and the leather carrying case for the 20-round mag-azines. The Swedish-Ks were different from the M-2 carbines, M-3 "grease guns," or AK-47s that we usually carried. I remember think-ing that the Swedish Ks were a bit too "pretty" for combat, but hell, we hadn't seen much combat during the last year.

Anyway, Jim and I figured there was not much sense having the weapons around if the magazines weren't loaded, so we stayed up late that night loading the magazines. When we finally went to bed, boxes of 9mm ammunition and tear gas grenades were still sitting on the living room table. Other than that, it was pretty much a normal night. I

felt good being back in Hue. I was back home.

The next morning, 31 January 1968, the first day of Tet, the Year of the Monkey, we were awakened at about 4:00 a.m. to the sound of gunfire and explosions in the dis-tance. The three of us who shared the house at No. 6 Nguyen Hue (Jim, Bob Ennis, and myself) gathered to find out what was hap-pening. According to our Nung guards out-side, the guard camp across the canal at Nam Giao was coming under attack, and they were noticeably concerned. To us, it wasn't that unusual because we'd had probing at-tacks every few night in the previous months as the Viet Cong probed outlying ARVN and Marine outposts. A couple months previously, the Viet Cong had attacked and overrun a Marine CAP (Combined Action Platoon) post just south of Hue. They killed the young Ma-rine CAP unit leader, a corporal, whom I had just met a couple weeks before.

While it wasn't particularly alarming, the sustained firefight indicated that it was something bigger than a probe. We continued to listen to the surreal pop-pop-popping of small arms fire. I thought how almost harmless it sounded, like firecrackers, not at all like gunfire as portrayed in the movies. We continued to monitor our radios, as we could hear the sounds of the firefight move west toward the Provincial Reconnaissance Unit (PRU) camp, located at a stately old French colonial compound called "Gerard."

We were cautiously monitoring the fighting, but not unduly alarmed. There were conflicting reports about whether "Gerard" was under attack up until then, but soon we got confirmation that it was coming under heavy attack. We continued to hear the sounds of small-arms fire and the "crump" of grenades and exploding mortar rounds coming from the two locations. The fighting was intensifying rapidly.

At about 7:00 a.m., Bob Hubbard, a Marine detailed to the embassy, and Howard Vaughn, a Marine sergeant advisor to the PRU, arrived by jeep at our house. They, too, had been monitoring the fighting and preparing to evacuate to the MACV compound about a mile away. Hubbard first wanted to go to the house of the Police Special Branch (PSB) advisor, located at No. 9 Phan Dinh Phung, to check on several people living there. Hubbard said they had not had any radio contact with them that morning. Hubbard and Jim departed through our backyard toward the Phu Cam Canal where the other house was located.

The sky was brightening, but the day was gray and overcast. A light mist shrouded the streets, and there was a slight chill in the air. Sergeant Vaughn and I went out to the front of the house to see if we could detect any activity. We did not have to wait long. We were standing by our gateposts when Sergeant Vaughn said he could see enemy soldiers running down Lam Son Street toward the provincial headquarters about 70 yards away. The soldiers were dressed in green uni-

forms, trousers rolled up above the knee, with each carrying a rucksack and a weapon. I looked out and could see small figures, crouched over, moving across my front about 100 yards away. It seemed like an endless stream of people running down the street.

Sergeant Vaughn said he was going to mark them with fire and let loose a short burst of fire from his M-16. Almost immediately, it was answered with automatic fire. Chips of stone flew off the gatepost, and Vaughn wheeled away from the post and fell to the ground. He spit up some blood, but otherwise there wasn't a lot of bleeding, so I could not tell how seriously he was wounded. He said he had taken one bullet below his left arm. He was coughing up blood, meaning the bullet had punctured a lung. I bent over Vaughn, but still did not know the seriousness of his wounds.

At that moment, a couple of mortar rounds struck the roof of our house and showered us with shards of broken tile. I asked Sergeant Vaughn if he could move into the house. He pushed himself up and stumbled, hunched over, into the house and fell, sprawling on the living room floor. I stayed outside a couple more minutes watching the NVA stream down the street, watching to see if they turned up the street toward our house. Things were getting more serious by the minute, yet how serious it was to become would not be known until later. Bob Ennis, who had been inside the house, went out to one of the jeeps to monitor radio transmissions. The radios we had in our jeeps were squawking with a steady stream of English. This was a dead giveaway that there were Americans nearby.

A few minutes later, about 7:30 a.m., Bob Hubbard and Jim Harris returned. They asked if I thought we could make a run for the MACV compound. I told them that a lot of enemy troops had already moved down toward the MACV compound and I did not think we could make it. Besides, I said, Sergeant Vaughn was seriously wounded. Harris

31

and Hubbard entered the house and went into one bedroom to check the condition of Vaughn and to try to establish radio contact with the MACV compound. I was across the living room in the other bedroom, watching the front door and a window on my side of the house. A few minutes later, I could see about a half dozen Viet Cong come from the adjacent house, No. 4 Nguyen Hue, cross in front of our house, and walk off out of sight...

About 8:30 a.m., I saw a grenade coming from somewhere to my right, out of my line of sight, and land on the seat of one of the jeeps parked outside our door. A second later there was an explosion and the jeep was engulfed in flames as the grenade touched off the gas tank. The second jeep soon followed the same fate. So much for using the jeeps to escape.

I don't know what happened to Bob Ennis. Frankly, in the confusion of the moment, I did not even think of him, as my attention was focused on the rapidly deteriorating situation. Several minutes went by, and I saw four VC parade a group of prisoners past our house, their hands above their heads in surrender. I recognized a couple of people as members of the IVS (International Volunteer Service), although I did not know their names. Also among the group were two of our Nung guards.

Around 9:30 a.m., one enemy soldier entered the house. He walked slowly toward the right side bedroom where Bob Hubbard and Jim Harris were. I was squatting down, pressed up against the door jam, hidden somewhat by a couch, watching the scene unfold. I looked over at Hubbard, who was watching the enemy approach. When the VC was about 10 feet from Bob, Bob stood up, and they both started firing on full automatic. It was like the gangster movies of the 1930s. Chips of wood were flying off the door around Hubbard, but Hubbard's bullets found their mark, and the VC wheeled, staggered a couple feet, and collapsed at our front door entrance. Somehow during this violent exchange, one of the French doors to

the bedroom where Hubbard was standing swung away from the wall, obscuring his view of the front door from that room. This was to have an impact on who engaged the next VC intruders. Bob came away without a scratch. Engaging the enemy at a distance is one thing, but a shootout at 10 feet was another thing. My adrenaline was pumping.

About 30 minutes passed before two other NVA would approach. I was surprised that our little firefight had not attracted more attention right after it happened—not that I was eager. The lead NVA glanced down at the body at the door but continued to enter the house slowly. The second NVA knelt down to examine the body more carefully. You could see that the NVA were used to jungle fighting, and their training did not prepare them for urban combat. I don't think either side was trained for urban warfare....The defender—in this case us—always has the advantage of surprise. This was certainly the case here, for I was crouched at the entry way to the left side bedroom watching the enemy enter. When he was about 10-12 feet away, I stood up, braced my back against the doorway, and opened fire on full automatic. I was so nervous that my first rounds hit the floor, and I remember walking the bullets up the enemy's leg to his body. He turned and collapsed. I raised my Swedish-K a bit and shot the other NVA soldier kneeling at the main doorway, and he went down right there.... [Notes that this is the first man he has killed.]

Another ten minutes or so went by, and the front doorway was rocked by an explosion from a RPG rocket, fired from across the street. The blast blew a hole in the wall, to the left of the front doorway. All I could remember was this cloud of red brick dust, and the blast picking me up and throwing me about 10 feet back into the bedroom. I was a bit shaken but unscathed as I quickly got up and crawled back into position at the doorway to the bedroom. I could now look out to the street through the open doorway and the hole blown through the wall, but I was feeling very vulnerable having to divide my attention between the front door and the windows of the left side bedroom, which had been blown open by the explosion. I assessed my position as being too untenable, so I scurried across the living room to join the others. Bob Hubbard was crouched near the window opening out to the street. Jim Harris was just inside the doorway I had just come through. Howard Vaughn was lying in the center of the room, fading in and out of consciousness. It looked very serious. I took up a position at the doorway, on the opposite side from Jim Harris.

I looked into the living room at the three bodies of the VC. I could see that a piece of the wall above where the RPG rocket had hit had come down and crashed on top of one of the bodies. If the fellow was not dead before, the piece of the wall surely finished him.

Hubbard continued to try to establish radio contact on the PRC-25—"Waverly Waver . . . Waverly Waver." . . . At one point, we could hear communications between some unidentified units. I thought it was the Air Cav because they referred to someone as "pony soldier," but we could not raise anyone. Unknown to us at the time, MACV had been under attack since 4:00 a.m., and they had changed frequencies and call signs.

It was about this time, about 10:00 a.m., that the NVA made a concerted effort to dislodge us. Several NVA ran and took cover just outside our front gate. I thought I saw one carrying a satchel charge and could only think of the death and destruction such charges made to the Marine CAP unit outside of Hue. A blast rocked the other side of the building. I could see one NVA soldier hiding behind the gatepost—the very same post that Vaughn was leaning against when he was wounded. I could see only a part of his head, so I aimed my Swedish-K at him and let loose a burst of fire. He screamed and went running down the street holding his head.

We looked out again and could see an NVA soldier scurry across the street with an RPG, and a couple seconds later, a second NVA followed carrying two rockets. I think the same

Photo courtesy of Mr. Rudy Enders
The Embassy House in Hue City after the Tet 1968 attack.

thought ran through each of our minds then, "Oh shit, here it comes." I think it was then that Bob Hubbard grabbed the bottle of Drambuie off the fireplace mantel, took a swig, and passed it around. Hell, it could be our last drink, so we each took a swallow. We quickly made a pact not to surrender, that we would fight to the death. I was not sure I liked that last promise, but we had to remain united.

A couple moments later, our house was rocked by the explosion as another RPG rocket hit our house. They had aimed at the other side of the house and again we were safe. I recall looking over at the windows and noticing that the plastic sheets we had used in the windows instead of glass was shredded, but that probably saved us from the injuries by flying glass. . . .

Just as suddenly as the attack began, things went quiet. We could hear the sound of helicopters outside, and I saw a Huey at treetop level, firing into the tree line. We were certain that this was the counterattack that we were waiting for and that the battle would soon be over. For the next half hour, things were deathly quiet. Suddenly, just outside our door, we could hear one of the wounded NVA, moan and cry. We were concerned that his cries would bring others, so Jim Harris grabbed a gun, crawled outside, and fired a couple rounds into him. Jim returned and said that he had taken care of him, but it wasn't more than a couple minutes later that the wounded man began moaning and crying again. We looked at each other, and Jim again went outside and rolled two grenades outside the front door— KRUMP, KRUMP. We were sure we had heard the last of him, but soon, the cries began again. Jim said, "Forget it, he's not real."

It had been a long, quiet period, and with the sight of the Hueys earlier, we were certain that things were drawing to a close. This seemed to match the enemy's M.O. [method of operations] of attacking during the night and early morning, then withdrawing during daylight. I don't think any of us thought that the NVA would hold Hue through daylight. However, we would wait until friendly troops could mop up and move through our area before we came out. Around 11:00 a.m., I saw a group of soldiers walking down the street. I thought they were friendly forces, probably ARVN because they had on green uniforms like what the ARVN wore and the lead individual was wearing a steel helmet.

Right about then, we took another rocket on our house. I thought it was a case of mistaken identity and told the others in the room, that I would try to identify us to these people. I called out "Hoa ky, Hoa ky," meaning "American, American." Almost immediately, it was answered by a burst of automatic fire. I dropped to the floor, hugging the tile, as bullets ripped through the wall. Bullets were coming through the brick wall not more than eight inches above my head, and I could see splinters of wood fly off the headboard of the bed.

Jim Harris, who had been squatting against the wall on the other side of the doorway, whispered "I'm hit!" I thought he meant a superficial wound and did not give it much thought until I saw him lean away from the wall, and it was covered in blood. Still, Jim seemed all right and not seriously wounded. We were to find out later that two rounds had gone through his right upper arm and

Another view of the Embassy House in Hue City after the Tet 1968 attack.

Photo courtesy of Mr. Rudy Enders

34

penetrated his back and lodged inside his right lung. Still thinking that it was mistaken identity, I called out again, "Hoa ky, Hoa Ky," which was answered by grenades and more small-arms fire.

It seemed as if the NVA were now in the other bedroom, as one grenade rolled into our room. Bob Hubbard dived for it and threw it back outside into the living room, where it exploded. A second grenade rolled and stopped at the door frame, about three feet from me. I plastered myself against the wall as the grenade exploded with a deafening blast. Except for a single small fragment of shrapnel on my left arm, I was not injured. I could smell a familiar odor, for a minute uncertain what it was, but soon realized it was tear gas from the stash of tear gas grenades we had left on the dining room table. Apparently, the explosions had ruptured some of those grenades, and the smoke was wafting into our room.

Reminiscent of the movie Butch Cassidy and the Sundance Kid, *Jim whispered, "Anymore good ideas?" He quickly added, "friendly or not, we're not going to take this" and produced two fragmentation grenades. Jim pulled the pins and nodded to me. I did not need further direction; I extended my Swedish-K into the doorway and sprayed a full magazine of bullets into the other room. As soon as I emptied the magazine, I pulled back and motioned to Jim, who rolled the two grenades into the other room. Two loud explosions in the next room seemed to silence things, and the house became quiet again.*

By now, it was obvious that we could not stay in the house. I was closest to the back door and nervously I pushed it open, fully expecting the NVA to be on the other side. I was "scared shitless," but I couldn't ask someone else to do this since I was there, closest to the door. I thought of the case of fragmentation grenades, just on the other side of the door. As I inched the door open, I was surprised to find that there was no one there and the coast was clear. I went to the back bathroom and came back to motion everyone to escape

through the rear window. Bob Hubbard helped Sergeant Howard through the window and hobble to one of the back houses. I think these were old servants' quarters, but they were empty now.

We took the last room in the row. Here we joined up with Bob Ennis and four of our Nung guards. Hubbard hid Vaughn under a concrete table, affording him good protection. The rest of us took up positions to cover the windows and doorways. We listened as the enemy moved through the main building and systematically blew up the house.

We stayed in this room for about an hour. We had no illusions that we could hold this position, but we had no idea where to move without stumbling into more NVA, so we stayed put. At about 12 noon, a rifle muzzle appeared outside our door. A shot came through the door, with the bullet striking Vaughn, this time blowing off his pinkie finger and breaking his leg. Hubbard yanked the door open and fired, killing three NVA. Hubbard pulled back, yelling that he was out of ammunition. I went to the door, ready to fire, but noticed the three NVA lying outside the room and no one else. I spied a grenade and extra magazines for an AK-47 on one of the bodies, and I stooped to take them. The grenade was knotted to his belt and I was trying to undo the knot.

Looking up, back at the main house, I made eye contact with a NVA soldier standing there in the bathroom window we had come through not that long ago. I think he was an NVA officer because he was wearing a tan pith helmet and seem to be in authority. We looked at each other for several seconds, and then I got up and casually walked around to the back of the building. I am convinced that he took me for a local VC because I was in civilian clothes and carrying an AK-47.

At the back of the building, I linked up with Hubbard and Vaughn. I motioned that I was going over the wall to check out the next compound. I rolled over the wall and ran to the nearest cover, which turned out to be a watershed. As I entered, I saw a body in the water trough. No sooner that I had gotten over that shock than the body rose up. It scared the pants off me, but I motioned him to be quiet, pushing him back down toward the water, and stepped out of the shed.

The only other place was a closet-like room with a small water trough. I went over to it, and it looked like a way to climb up to the attic crawl space, where I thought we could hide. I waved to Hubbard to follow, and the two of us hoisted Vaughn up the wall and pushed him up. He let out a muffled scream, and then we heard a thud and moan. It soon became apparent that what I thought was an attic was only the other side of the wall, and we had just dropped Vaughn over the wall. Hubbard climbed over and I quickly followed. On the other side, there was another water trough, and I kneeled on the rim, facing a window and door. Vaughn was lying on the floor. Bob had taken up a position looking out another window.

This was the first chance that we had to regroup. During the last skirmish, everyone scattered, and now only Hubbard, Vaughn, and I were together. We did not know where Jim Harris and Bob Ennis had gone, nor did we know where our Nung guards went. I do not remember how long we stayed there. We could hear some activity going on around us, but we did not see anything. Sometime later that afternoon, I saw a Vietnamese outside our building. He wandered about for a while and then came to the door and peered through the crack, straight at me. I was still squatting on the water trough, with a weapon cradled in my arms. I stared back, but otherwise did not move. I was certain he saw me, but I wasn't certain whether he would report our presence. Luck was with us, and nothing came of this incident.

As night fell, I moved into the small room with Hubbard. He had already moved Vaughn and slid him under the bed in the room. Hubbard faced out the small openings to the back, while I sat in the doorway looking out the window. We had made it through

day one. It seemed like forever.

Some time during that first night, I suddenly heard voices coming from directly in front of me, and in the faint light coming in the window I could see two figures. I think they were a man and a woman. I do not know how or when they came into our building, but they were suddenly there, not more than four feet away. I called to them in my limited Vietnamese, saying that I was a friend and not to be afraid, all the while slowly moving toward them, hand over hand. By the time I reached the window, they were gone. I never found out who they were or how they got in and out without us hearing anything. The rest of the night and the next day were uneventful, and Bob and I kept our same positions. Vaughn continued to fade in and out of consciousness, and we did not know how long he would last.

On the second night, 1 February 1968, Bob noticed two figures moving outside. By their movements, we could tell they were Jim Harris and Bob Ennis. We called to them in a whisper and guided them into our building through a back door. They soon joined us and told us of their story of taking refuge in the main building of this compound. They said that they hid in a closet, while just outside their door less than five feet away, NVA soldiers gathered and chatted in the dark. This night, they decided to sneak past the NVA soldiers and try to escape, when we called to them. They joined us in our small room. Bob Hubbard, Jim Harris and Bob Ennis sat on the bed, Sergeant Vaughn was lying under the bed, and I sat across from them on a bag of rice. Vaughn was still alive but getting weaker, slipping in and out of consciousness. We shared a bar of brown sugar and an apple that we had taken from the worship altar and water from our water source.

Jim Harris had lost quite a bit of blood and was weak. Bob Hubbard rolled Jim on his wounded side to drain the blood from his good lung into the bad lung and gave Jim water. By the next day, Jim had recuperated much of his strength, but he was getting increasingly concerned about his wounds—that he might lose his right arm to gangrene. We were fortunate to have some food and a ready source of water. No one got sick, and we quietly urinated into a small bottle and then poured it into an urn full of rice. The room was small, about four feet by six feet, but being together kept our spirits up.

Throughout the next few days, we saw no other people. We only heard sporadic firing nearby. Frequently we would hear a loud gun go off, followed by automatic fire. The firing would build in intensity and then gradually taper off. I wasn't sure if it was antiaircraft fire or other defensive fires. Often this firing sequence was preceded by a whippoorwill-like birdcall, to the point where I thought it might be a signal. Then again, I thought to myself that perhaps I'd been watching too many war movies where people would use birdcalls as recognition signals. To this day, I do not know what if there was any significance to the birdcall, or if it were an actual birdcall.

Sergeant Vaughn was getting increasingly weaker. He lay under the bed, not making a sound. We knew that we could not move him, and the best bet was that friendly forces would recapture this part of the city and we would be able to medevac him. We were still confident that U.S. forces would win this area back. It was just a matter of time before they would, though whether it would be in time to save Vaughn was more in question. Thinking back, I cannot recall if he was conscious at any time during the last two days we were in the room. If we had to move quickly, the decision was made that we would hide Vaughn under the bed. If we tried to move him, he would surely die.

By the third day (2 February), we were wondering when the U.S. forces would recapture Hue. Where were they? Jim was getting increasingly nervous about his wounds. He feared they would become gangrenous and he would lose his arm. We were becoming desperate. We were thinking of crazy plans

for escape. One plan had us find the aluminum wrapper from cigarette packs to fashion a mirror to signal friendly aircraft. Another plan had me pretend to be a VC and march the others at gunpoint toward a checkpoint and then rush the guards and blast our way through. We had been watching too many movies, and we realized that the chances for success were slim to none.

Amidst this reverie, we heard a commotion outside our door. We quickly bolted the door and listened as a number of NVA soldiers entered our building and interrogated a local Vietnamese, just outside our room. There was a lot of yelling, screaming, crying, and an occasional shot. It was confusion. The best we could make out was that the NVA found Sergeant Vaughn's blood-stained clothes, which we had stripped off him when we first came into the building. The only barrier between us and the NVA was a seven-foot-high concrete wall, open at the top, and a flimsy wood-and-tin door held shut by a small bolt lock. We knew it was a simple matter for the NVA to kick down our door or throw a grenade over the wall.

We made hand signs as to who would do what. We quieted our breathing, and the sweat was streaming off our faces. Suddenly, someone tried our door. It was obvious that the door was locked from the inside, and we were certain someone would kick the door in. We readied ourselves to blast our way out. We waited for what seemed like forever, but nothing happened, and just as suddenly, the NVA left. We all let out a huge sigh of relief. We could never figure out what brought them to our house and why they suddenly left, but we were grateful that we did not have a firefight in such close quarters.

The relief of that close call was still with us the next morning. Someone had found a can of sweetened evaporated milk, and we were trying to figure out how to open it when we heard footsteps. This was about 11:00 a.m. A number of NVA marched into the house, straight to our door, and kicked it down. Bob Hubbard rushed to the door and sprayed the room with his Swedish-K. After a couple seconds, he pulled back, saying he was out of ammo. I jumped into the doorway with an AK-47 and fired one round. I thought that I had placed the AK on full automatic, but much to my surprise, it was on semi-auto. I stood there white knuckled, and only one round came out. I quickly realized my mistake and pulled the trigger in rapid succession. The two NVA soldiers who barged in were lying on the floor, but we did not wait around to see who else was there, so we bolted out the door.

We ran to the corner of the compound and climbed over, through what I believe was the Montagunard Center. It wasn't until later that we learned that an NVA Regiment had made it their headquarters. We skirted the compound, climbed over another wall, and into a garage. It was then that I realized that, in the heat of the firefight, we had left Sergeant Vaughn behind. A couple of us were ready to go back, but after a brief discussion, we figured we would never be able to get him out alive and that his best chance was to remain hidden under the bed in the house. (We were convinced that the NVA couldn't hold the city much longer and our side would recapture the city soon.) We weren't even sure he was still alive. He had not made a sound for the last couple days. To this day, I am haunted by the question whether we did the right thing.

We left the garage and slowly made our way, half submerged, down a water-filled canal. We quietly passed a woman cooking in her backyard. I can remember thinking that she could not help but have noticed us, or she purposely avoided looking at us....The canal came up to a rusted barbwire fence. On the other side was a road—and our way out. We broke a hole through the fence and slithered through. I ended up at a culvert in the road. I quickly slid into the culvert. As I crawled forward, I could see mosquitoes on the water and thought to myself, "Oh shit, after all this, now I am going to get bitten and die of malaria." But that thought was quickly pushed from my mind as the culvert

narrowed and I found my nose under water. I quickly turned over on my back so my nose would be out of the water as I squeezed out the other end. Good thing I was all of about 125 pounds and could get through. Being exposed on the side of the road, I ran forward, hid in a ditch, and waited for the others.

Unbeknownst to me, they had decided that they would never get through the culvert and had run across the road and south toward the Phu Cam district, expecting me to catch up. I, however, got turned around and found myself headed back toward the city. I recognized a compound that was just down the road from our house. It was the public works department for the city. The roads were empty, though I could still hear gunfire in the distance. As soon as I heard a break in the shooting, I pushed up, ran across the road into the compound, and climbed up into a concrete water tower.

There I felt I was safe and could dry off. I was soaked from crawling through the canal, and I was shivering as the temperatures dropped. I stripped off my clothes and laid them out to dry, just sitting in the dry water tower in my underwear. No sooner did I strip down than it started to rain, so reluctantly I put back on my wet clothes. I was cold, miserable, and hungry, so I decided to approach the Vietnamese in the compound. I had no better ideas.

I jumped down and started to run but thought better of it, so I slowed to a walk and walked across the compound to a Vietnamese woman. Using my scant Vietnamese, I explained that I was an American and that I wanted to know what the situation was. The woman ushered me into her house and told me that the NVA had overrun all of Hue and Phu Bai. She gave me some rice mixed with some red sauce, and I wolfed it down. I never found out what the red sauce was, but at the time, it tasted great. I wasn't sure what I would do, but I wanted to get out of the wet clothes, so I asked for something dry to wear. They gave me a white shirt and a pair of blue schoolboy trousers and a pair of shower shoes. Nervously, they took my clothes and buried them in the yard, but not until I retrieved my wallet and dog tags. As I started to leave, they told me that I could not leave the compound since the NVA were everywhere and I would be killed or captured for sure. Instead, they led me to a small pen that best I could tell was an old pigsty. They motioned that I should hide there.

The pigsty was low, and I could not stand up, so I sat leaning against a wooden side. The next couple days were uneventful. The family brought me food twice a day, and I occupied myself doing isometric exercises to keep from cramping up. At other times, I looked for things to keep me occupied. Once I found some wire and spent time sewing the buttons back on my shirt. On the second day, the husband came over to me and handed me a rusty knife blade. He explained that during the night, the NVA had come to him and asked if they could cut through to the next compound, through where I was hiding. Wanting to give me something to defend myself, he gave me this knife. I took one look and thought it would be useless. It was rusted and dull, and I couldn't even use it to cut my own throat, if it came to that. But I thanked him nonetheless.

Sitting in the pigsty, I continued to hear sporadic gunfire throughout the city, along with the staccato of automatic fire. Increasingly, I could hear artillery rounds going overhead, which I assumed were from Phu Bai.

By the second day, my existence was turning into routine. I was trying to keep myself entertained when an artillery shell exploded less than 30 feet from me. All I could remember was that everything turned to slow motion, and I could see the fireball and the billowing cloud of red brick dust move toward me. The force knocked me over, and all I could think of was, "Oh shit, it's going to break my leg!" The walls of the pigsty and the overhead corrugated roofing collapsed on top of me. I pushed off the ground and back into an upright sitting position, only to

see another fireball, almost at precisely the same spot, and another wave of red brick dust knocked me over again.

As I pushed back upright again, I checked myself and noticed that I was still in one piece—no broken leg. I did have a small wound on my head, probably from the falling roof and timbers, but the building fell in such a way as to create a small lean-to—very much like a 1950s nuclear bomb shelter—and I was lying in this lean-to. I checked around and noticed gouges in the cinder blocks next to me. I did not recall seeing them before the blasts, but I couldn't say for sure that they were caused by the blasts. If the latter, that I survived was a miracle. As it was, it was a miracle anyway.

That day, for the first time, the Vietnamese family did not bring any food to me. I fashioned a drinking cup from a discarded C-rations tin and caught rain water dripping from the corrugated roofing for drinking water. I would simply collect the water, allow for sediment to settle to the bottom of the tin, and sip the "clean" water off the top. It worked well, especially since the weather cooperated with a light drizzle all day. It wasn't until the next day that someone from the Vietnamese family came around looking for some roofing material that they realized that I had not died in the explosions. When I waved to them, the person blanched, looked as if he'd seen a ghost, and scurried away. He soon returned with a bandage and some food, which was greatly welcomed. Later that day, they brought me food again.

I continued to "live" in my makeshift shelter. My only concern now was the threat of rats, and I wrapped the mosquito net that the family had given me tightly around my body to ward off any rat attacks, as well as to keep warm. No rats came. They were probably too smart to venture out during this fighting. I only mention it because it reflects my state of mind—I may survive the fighting, but something else would do me in, like malaria or rats, or something else.

On 7 February, the firefights grew in intensity, and I could hear American English on the other side of the wall. It was the Marines, and I would hear, "Don't worry, the Marines are here," "U.S. Marines," and other such phrases, occasionally punctuated with gunfire. A lot sounded like so much bravado, but to me it was a welcome sound and hope. It was now only a matter of minutes, I thought. It turned out to be a couple hours before the Marines came through the hole in the wall made by the two artillery shells. Now my concern was how do I come out without being mistaken for a VC and get shot. I got out my dog tags and my military ID and held them in my hand. When I could actually see them, I called, "Hey Marines, Captain Lau, U.S. embassy. I'm coming out."

A voice called back, "Come on out. We've been looking for you." Holding my military ID card and my dog tags, I crawled out of my shelter and introduced myself to Captain J.T. Irons of the Marine ITT team, resplendent in his handlebar moustache. He was ugly, but a most beautiful sight.

Shortly thereafter, Captain Irons escorted me back to the MACV compound. I must have been quite a sight—an eight-day growth on my face, a white shirt and blue schoolboy trousers, and shower shoes. The guard at the MACV compound called out to us as we entered, "Hey, he can't go in there!" Capt. Irons yelled back, "He's okay. He's a Marine captain." We continued walking, and soon I was greeted by my chief, Billy G. Melton. He greeted me with a big smile and a pat on the back. It was great to see him.

That day, several others were to make it back to friendly lines. Dave Harper and John Coffey walked in. They had a similar harrowing story to tell, but that's their story. I also learned that Jim Harris had made it down to Phu Bai and had been medevaced to the U.S. Bob Ennis took refuge at the Voice of America Station just south of Hue, was safe, and would later be exfiltrated out of the area. Sadly, Bob Hubbard had been killed about three days earlier as they crossed the bridge to Phu Cam District. He had been shot at close range and likely died instantly.

Over the next couple days, I identified the bodies of Tom Gompertz, Tom Krause, and Jeff Lundstedt as their bodies were brought in. A Marine was driving one of the USAID Ford Scouts and would come screeching around the corner to the MACV compound, horn blaring, and I would go down to ID the bodies. I got to dread the sound of the horn since I knew it meant bodies. But I thought it was the least I could do, to help get their bodies back to their families. I would have wanted them to do that for me if the roles were reversed.

For the next month or more, we tracked others who were missing, and I brought back the bodies of Sergeant Howard Vaughn and a USAID officer, Steve Miller. I found Sergeant Vaughn's body in a ditch outside the building where we were hiding. I looked, but I did not see any more wounds than those he had suffered that first day. All told, 10 people from the embassy team in Hue were killed during or as a result of the fighting in Hue—Bob Hubbard, Howard Vaughn, Tom Gompertz, Tom Krause, Jeff Lundstedt, Steve Miller, and four others. Gene Weaver was captured and ended up as a POW in North Vietnam for seven years. Tom Ragsdale was captured but died of dysentery along the Ho Chi Minh trail. Sol Godwin and Steve Haukness were never found or their whereabouts never determined. They will all be remembered by me as long as I live.[29]

Ray Lau left the Marine Corps and went on to a distinguished career with the CIA.

Sergeant Rodney H. Pupuhi: I Corps, Post-Tet 1968

Sergeant Rodney H. Pupuhi, a native of Hawaii, enlisted in the Marine Corps in 1954 and served until 1957 when he left the active Marine Corps and joined the Marine Corps Reserve. In 1962, his reserve infantry unit was reorganized as the 6th Force Reconnaissance Company, and he began several years of intensive training in parachuting, scuba diving, and other reconnaissance skills.

Sergeant Rodney H. Pupuhi, second on the left in civilian clothes, with unit leaders of Quang Nam Provincial Reconnaissance Unit during his tour in 1968.

As a highly trained reconnaissance Marine with a strong urge to test his skills in combat, Sergeant Pupuhi decided to rejoin the active Marine Corps in 1965 and volunteer to go to Vietnam. He served in a detachment of the 1st Reconnaissance Battalion assigned to the 5th Marines in I Corps. When the 1st Reconnaissance Battalion deployed to Vietnam, Sergeant Pupuhi joined the battalion at Chu Lai. In March 1968 he received orders to report to the PRU as the replacement for Sergeant William A. Polchow, the Marine PRU advisor in Hoi An, Quang Nam Province, who was killed in action near Hoi An on 23 January 1968, just a few days prior to the Tet Offensive.

Pupuhi's introduction to the PRU started with a jeep ride from the 1st Reconnaissance Battalion's base at Camp Reasoner on the eastern slope of Hill 327 west of Da Nang City to a meeting with his "CIA contact." The CIA officer drove "an old beat-up 4x4 Ford Bronco, wore a shoulder holster, and was dressed in civilian clothes." He drove Pupuhi to the embassy house in Da Nang City, which Pupuhi remembered as "a villa surrounded by barbwire with four guard towers at each corner of the compound and manned by Vietnamese guards in camouflage uniforms." Inside the villa, he was introduced to a U.S. Marine "Colonel Moon,"[30] who welcomed him aboard and gave him strict instructions about who he was to take orders from and what he could and could not do while assigned to the PRU.

Sergeant Pupuhi was quickly processed into the program. He had his picture taken for a Vietnamese police ID and was told the ID identified him as an officer, not an enlisted man. The ID was signed by a South Vietnamese general, whom he believed was the senior Vietnamese officer in Quang Nam Province. He was assigned a Mitsubishi Jeep and sent to the CIA armory to sign for his personal weapons, a Swedish K submachine gun, a Browning 9-millimeter automatic pistol, and a 25-caliber

Berretta pistol. He was also issued a case of ammunition for each weapon.

Pupuhi was given $200 to buy civilian clothes at the Freedom Hill PX and then, after a few days, he was flown to Saigon's Tan Son Nhut air base on an Air America flight from the Da Nang air base. In Saigon, he was briefed by a CIA officer called John in one of the upper floors of the American embassy, then he was driven to the MACV headquarters, where he was briefed by a woman Marine major who was in charge of the section that would take care of his personal records and pay.

While in Saigon, Sergeant Pupuhi was given a room at the Duc Hotel, which was leased to the CIA for the agency's exclusive use. He, along with three other new PRU advisors, received two weeks of training from a CORDS instructor who seemed to go out of his way to stress the danger awaiting them. Pupuhi also spent a few days at the CIA training facility at Vung Tau before he was sent north to take over his PRU teams in Hoi An. His instruction at Vung Tau was cut short because of the necessity to replace the PRU advisor in Hoi An, Sergeant Pulchow, who had been killed during a combined PRU-Vietnamese Navy operation against the VCI. When he left Vung Tau, he was told that his immediate mission was "to restore the unit at Hoi An."

In Hoi An, Pupuhi lived in what was called "the little embassy," a very large white one-story villa with an adjacent warehouse in which were stored "uniforms, web gear, boots, weapons, and anything else needed for war." Twenty Chinese Nung guards protected the house, with four of them on duty at all times. In addition to Pupui, there were three other Americans living in the villa. They were the POIC, who was a retired U.S. Air Force colonel, and two Marine lieutenants, one of whom was in charge of the Rural Development Program.

The POIC had several Vietnamese working for him, but they did not live in the house; they only worked there doing administrative jobs. According to Pupuhi, these Vietnamese workers "were very dependable and loyal" and appeared to enjoy the complete trust of the POIC since they often typed classified letters and reports for him.

Pupuhi's right-hand man was his interpreter, Bu Than Ming, whom Pupuhi described as "a tall, lanky Vietnamese man who wore an Air Force baseball cap, soft-type flak jacket, skin tight trousers, and pilot's sunglasses." Ming had worked as an interpreter for the U.S. Air Force before coming to the PRU, and he spoke English fluently. Ming worked with Pupuhi to resurrect the Quang Nam PRU from a force of only seven members to over 100 in just a few short weeks. He helped Pupuhi to create the personnel folders for each PRU recruit, to have them receive their initial medical exams at the German hospital in Hoi An, and to make sure the new recruits were fed and clothed properly and their families cared for.

Since the PRU was newly formed—or more

Sergeant Pupuhi on the right with a Swedish K submachine gun. On the left is his interpreter, Mr. Ming. Taken in Quang Nam Province in 1968.
Photo courtesy of GySgt Rodney H. Pupuhi

accurately, reformed—Pupuhi spent a lot of time training his new recruits so they would be able to begin patrolling and conducting counter-VCI missions. This included a lot of time teaching them the proper care and cleaning of their individual and crew-served weapons, scouting and patrolling techniques, land navigation, marksmanship, first aid, and communications. His PRU was equipped with M-16 rifles, M-79 grenade launchers, 45-caliber Colt automatic pistols, and M-60 machine guns. He conducted a weapons inspection every morning before training. They also had two 4x4 Honda trucks, which were inadequate for all the PRU members to ride in at one time. This resulted in the vehicles often being "packed like sardines with standing room only" when they were used to transport the PRU on a mission.

Most PRU missions involved night ambushes near or in VC-controlled villages.

Pupuhi recalled that only once did they encounter a VC effort to penetrate the Quang Nam PRU. A VC had married into the family of a PRU member and used this family connection to enlist in the PRU. However, since the PRU had several former VC among their ranks, they soon became suspicious of this individual and began an internal investigation into his background. His family members provided information that cast doubt on his loyalty, and objects were found among his personal effects that proved he was in contact with the VC.

A few days later, the PRU took the VC spy on a patrol near Hoi An. When the patrol returned, they informed Pupui that the spy had been killed in a contact with the enemy and they had buried him in a shallow grave approximately a mile from the PRU compound. The spy's family was informed that he had died while on patrol, and they were given the normal death gratuity that all the families of PRU members killed in action were given. Pupuhi was suspicious about the death of the VC spy and cautioned the PRU members that in the future, they were never to take summary action against any person, regardless of the evidence. Pupuhi reported the incident to the

province chief for his action but never heard anything further regarding it.[31]

Sergeant Pupuhi retired from the Marine Corps in 1973 with the rank of gunnery sergeant and went on to complete a second career with the Hawaii State Sheriff's Office.

First Lieutenant Douglas P. Ryan: I Corps, 1968-69

Douglas P. Ryan was a first lieutenant serving in Vietnam as the S-2 of 1st Battalion, 4th Marines, when he received orders to report to Da Nang City to take over as officer in charge (OIC) of the five provincial PRU teams in I Corps. He served with the PRU in several capacities from October 1968 until August 1969. The following are excerpts from an e-mail sent to the author by Ryan that relate his experiences with the PRU:

Initially I was based in Da Nang City and placed in charge of the five provincial PRU units in I Corps which were commanded by Marine NCOs and SNCOs. These provinces were stretched from the Demilitarized Zone to the beginning of the Central Highlands in the south. From north to south, they were: Quang Tri, Thua Thien, Quang Nam, Quang Tin, and Quang Ngai. After a month in this job, the "powers that be" raised the rank level of the PRU advisors in I Corps. I was replaced by U.S. Army Major Raupach, and the enlisted province PRU advisors were replaced by officers. As a result, I was sent to Tam Ky to take over the PRU unit for Quang Tin Province. I spent eight months in Quang Tin, and then during the last two months of my tour, I was sent north to replace a U.S. Army officer in Quang Tri Province as the PRU advisor for that province.

We had about 110 PRU members in Quang Tin Province, and they came from many sources. Some came from the PRU predecessor unit, the Counter Terrorist Team, while others were hired from workers who had been involved in the construction of the U.S. Marine base at Chu Lai. They had varied backgrounds and education levels. I don't think we had any former VC or criminals in the unit, an "urban legend" that often was ascribed to the PRU. The Quang Tri PRU was much larger than the Quang Tin PRU, but I am not sure of the exact numbers because they were disbursed throughout the province. My guess is they had approximately 150 men.

I lived in the "embassy houses" in both Tam Ky and Quang Tri, which I shared with my POICs and assorted contractors who advised the Provincial Interrogation Center, the Police Special Branch, and the Census Grievance Program. While I was in Tam Ky, I had a deputy PRU advisor assigned with me, Gunnery Sergeant Sean Kennedy. The PRU in Quang Tri did not have a second American assigned to the PRU as deputy advisor.

When I am asked the question, "Was your unit effective in their mission of rooting out the VCI?" I can only reply that we may never know the answer to that question. I say this because the first thing I needed to do when I took over my PRU was to transition the unit from serving a dual role of gathering military intelligence and VCI intelligence to focusing on targeting VCI for capture. We had very little PIOCC help because the Phoenix family of intelligence gathers kept their information to themselves and did not share operational leads with the PRU as they were supposed to. We had good success in capturing several significant VCI, but it was done using PRU intelligence assets exclusively.

We often found that our small three-man cells had to fight their way in to get VCI because the VCI were normally protected by party security cadre and VC guerrillas. I think we were effective because we were focused. The lingering question is whether or not the targeting was accurate and not just score-settling or non-political activity, such as debt collection, "blue on blue" political feuding between the VNQDD and the Dai Vet, or simply factional fighting within these political parties.

The PRU was much better when it was concentrated than when it was farmed out to the districts to fend for themselves. We were encouraged to do this while I was there, but it did not work for us, primarily because of command and control problems and logistics difficulties. Some of the districts were in "Indian Country," particularly Tien Phuoc district in Quang Tin and the districts in western Quang Tri, so it was much better when we were concentrated in central compounds in Tam Ky and Quang Tri.

I think the main strengths of the PRU were courage, focus, and agility. Their weaknesses involved marksmanship and tactical training. We spent a lot of time training to overcome these two weaknesses. We also concentrated our training on helicopter raids, the use of supporting arms, communications, and fire control. While I was there, we developed a corps of local hospital-trained PRU corpsmen, greatly improved our communications capabilities, and worked on fire and maneuver tactics. They had outstanding movement skills and got the job done. They were especially adept at conducting a raid and consolidating an objective once it was taken. Several PRU cells received outstanding training at the PRU National Training Center at Vung Tau. Operationally, we did much better when we operated alone rather than with U.S. or other Vietnamese forces.

As far as what were the best and worse intelligence sources for my PRU, I can only say that my strong suit was infantry operations and not intelligence gathering. I never had a handle on intelligence sourcing. I do know that the PRU developed their own intelligence on targets, and it must have been good because we had a very good track record of VCI captures and kills. Our best intelligence was intelligence acted upon within hours of receiving it.

I got along well with the province chief in Quang Tin, and so did the PRU. He needed us for perimeter security because we shared the provincial compound with him. I had access to him and cleared some of our operations with him, but I never fully trusted him. I don't believe the PRU *chief had any relationship with him.*

Our most successful operation involved one that was supported by the U.S. 1st Cavalry Division. They provided a five-helicopter package for us, which included two Huey transports, two gunships, and an observation helicopter. Responding to excellent intelligence, we surrounded a village and picked up a number of middle-level VCI and captured several local guerrillas and weapons. We also killed 29 VC that day.

Some of our more creative operations were not successful, such as night raids on VC political meetings where we disrupted the meeting but were unable to secure any prisoners. On one operation we had precise information on the location of a VCI cadre—the bed he would be sleeping in—but when we walked into the village at night and approached his house, we were noticed and had to retreat under fire to a CIDG Special Forces camp using preplanned single-shot artillery fire behind us so as to deter the pursuing VC.

On another occasion, we went after 20 reported district-level VCI, but when we approached the target, we found ourselves in the middle of a local battalion-sized VC unit, and it took us all day and a lot of air support to get our PRU out. We lost eight PRU killed in action on this operation and did not come back with any prisoners.

The lesson we learned from these operations was the VCI tended to work and sleep with sizeable protection forces, and this often made it very difficult to capture VCI with a small PRU force.[32]

After leaving active duty in 1969, Lieutenant Ryan worked for the CIA from 1972 to 1980 and with the United States Foreign Service from 1980 through 2003. He continues to work part time for the State Department's Political-Military Bureau.

Captain Frederick J. Vogel: I Corps, 1969

A 1965 graduate of the U.S. Naval Academy,

Frederick J. (Fred) Vogel served from February to September 1969 as the PRU advisor in Hoi An, Quang Nam Province, I Corps. The following are comments derived from two e-mail interviews he provided to the author:

I was self-recruited for the PRU. I had heard about the PRU from another officer and went to Da Nang to the PRU Regional Office to check on available assignments. There were none at the time, but when I returned from extension leave (a voluntary six-month extension to my normal 13-month tour of duty in Vietnam), a position had opened up. I learned later that the former PRU advisor in Hoi An had been reassigned rather suddenly because of a conflict with the ROIC.

Historically, the Quang Nam PRU was the "bad boy" of the PRU Program. It was originally created at the same time as the country-wide program, but in about 1967 or 1968, it was disbanded and not reconstituted for about a year or so. This was all before my time, but the story of its demise and resurrection was described to me in detail by U.S. officials but never mentioned by the Vietnamese.

The problem for the PRU—and for Quang Nam Province in general—was the often violent power struggle between the Dai Vet and the VNQDD political parties for control of the province. These two political parties probably spent more time fighting each other than they did the Lao Dong Party and its VC minions. The provincial capital, Hoi An, was in a constant state of turmoil as a result. The PRU were naturally involved, and there were rifts within the unit itself along party lines. In fact, the day I arrived in Hoi An to take over the unit, we had to medevac a PRU member who had just been seriously wounded in a barracks firefight.

To go back further in time, at some point in the mid-1960s, the internal conflict had become so serious, and the PRU so badly diverted from its stated mission, that the PRU Program management in Saigon decided to disband the Quang Nam unit entirely. By this time, the Quang Nam PRU was conducting more operations against the various legal South Vietnamese parties than against the VCI. This included assassinations. The POIC at the time, in a moment of colossal bad judgment, actually called for a formation of the PRU in the POIC compound, told them they were a bunch of thugs and malcontents, and then fired the lot of them on the spot. This did not go over well at all. A firefight erupted in the compound with the former PRU trying heroically to make one more assassination—of the POIC himself! The hapless fellow did manage to extricate himself, but that was the end of the Quang Nam PRU. The POIC was transferred out of the province, replaced, and Quang Nam went for one or two years without a PRU. When it was once again established, it was put under the leadership of a RD cadre lieutenant and staffed with all new members, and many if not most had little combat experience.

The reconstituted PRU had an uphill struggle to regain any momentum in the fight against the VCI. Although there was very little coordination with or overt control over the PRU by the province chief, clearly everything the PRU did was cleared at province headquarters level. Unfortunately, it was a one-way street, with no real guidance or direction by the province and no intelligence provided by the Vietnamese side. The atmosphere was one of the provinces trying to rein in the activities of the Dai Vet and the VNQDD, as they might have been exercised through the PRU. As a result, the PRU were somewhat passive and had to be constantly pressured by me to be more proactive in developing actionable intelligence and launching operations against the VCI.

I wish I could say something more positive about the support we received from the POIC. Although he and his staff were very supportive, they really did not relate to combat operations as such. I do not recall a single intelligence lead developed by the POIC that resulted in a PRU operation. It was virtually entirely up to me to ferret out the sources of actionable intelligence. For the most part,

this came from the interrogation of POWs who were held at province level or had been captured by the U.S. military.

I was criticized at times for relying too much on the U.S. operations, but this did seem to work for the otherwise directionless PRU. Our services were often called upon by the American military for support, but just as often they attempted to use the PRU for police-type missions. Once I had corrected the misapprehension of the American officers, they were amenable to allowing the PRU to operate more or less independently when a military operation penetrated VC territory. This was not always a good thing. I recall one such operation on Go Noi Island south of Da Nang when we were totally cut off and effectively abandoned by elements of the U.S. Americal Division. We ended up in a running gunfight with VC main-force units as we made our way back to safety across the sand dunes. We inflicted a good number of casualties on the VC and captured a few, with no losses to ourselves, but it was a bit tight for a while.

One other source of intelligence served us well, and it was developed by the PRU themselves. About midway through my PRU tour, two young male students came to our compound in Hoi An and volunteered information about a VCI effort to suborn their village in central Quang Nam Province. They were very concerned and volunteered to accompany us on an operation to eliminate the VC threat to their village.

My Gunny, Gunnery Sergeant Richard Henrickson, who had come to the PRU from the infantry, later described this operation as the best he had witnessed in two tours of duty in Vietnam. We first enlisted the aid of the U.S. Marine battalion in the area of the village and then we set up a cordon of the village. Under the cover of darkness, we entered the village. At first light we sprang our trap. There was a bit of fighting at first, but for the most part, the VCI attempted to simply lay low and hope to wait out the operation.

With our two students, however, we were

able to identify virtually every VCI cadre in the village, and soon we had arrested all of them and began to interrogate them on the spot. The captured VCI were surprisingly co-operative. They gave us everything we wanted to know. We were able to exploit the leads these captives, gave us and they led to further captures. We offered to reward the two young students, but they refused, saying they only wanted to protect their village. I heard later that they went to Saigon to further their studies.

As my tour with the PRU came to an end, we made some changes in the PRU leadership. I was allowed to approach the province chief and ask him to return the PRU chief to the RD Program and to have his deputy take over the unit. The new PRU chief was a much more aggressive combat leader, but I departed before I could assess any results of his new leadership style. I can only surmise that it was more effective than under the old chief. [33]

After leaving the active Marine Corps, Captain Vogel joined the Marine Corps Reserve, where he attained the rank of colonel. As a civilian, he went on to a distinguished career with both the CIA and the U.S. Department of State.

A Typical Operational Scenario: Tay Ninh, 1970

Although it would be difficult to characterize PRU operations as "typical" in any respect, the following scenario is based on the author's own experience as a PRU advisor in Tay Ninh Province in III Corps and is taken from a monthly report filed with the PRU Headquarters in Saigon in early 1970 just before the invasion of Cambodia. It describes how the Phoenix program and the PRUs functioned in the latter stages of the U.S. involvement in the Vietnam War just a few months before MACV removed its military advisors from the PRU Program:

My operations officer, Mr. Tho, came to the embassy house next to the MACV Advisory Compound in Tay Ninh City for his usual

Photo courtesy of Col Andrew R. Finlayson
Capt Andrew R. Finlayson, left, with members of the Tay Ninh Provincial Reconnaissance Unit near Nui Ba Den Mountain in 1969.

0900 morning meeting with me. As was our daily custom, Mr. Tho was escorted from the front gate to the front porch of the embassy house by one of our Nung guards, and then we began to review the results of the previous day's activities and discuss any future plans. We met on the porch of our house because it was cool in the shade there, we could share a cup of coffee, and it was secure.

Our security officer never allowed any Vietnamese or American visitors inside the embassy house unless they possessed a security clearance and were cleared for entry in advance of their visit. The CIA officers in Tay Ninh Province—The Provincial Officer in Charge (POIC), the Police Special Branch (PSB) Advisor, the Provincial Interrogation Center (PIC) Advisor, and the PRU advisor— all had their offices in the house, and many

47

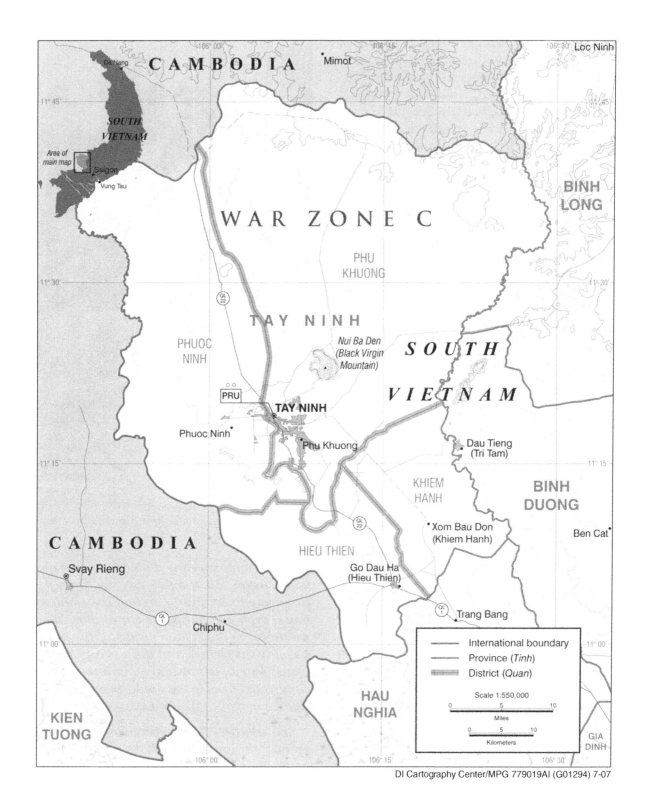

highly classified subjects were discussed there. In addition, classified working documents were frequently on desks in the embassy house offices during the working day so it was important for access to the villa to be tightly restricted. The embassy house had an annex behind the villa in which several Vietnamese workers had their offices. These annex offices were used by our Vietnamese financial manager and his clerk, our radio

48

operator, and our two interpreters during the work day.

Mr. Tho informed me that a PRU source, the family member of a PRU soldier, had reported to him that a commo-liaison cadre (secret courier used to transport VC documents) working for the Tay Ninh Provincial Party Committee would be traveling to the An Tan Border Station on the Cambodian border the next day. He further stated that this commo-liaison agent could well be carrying documents for the enemy's Central Office South Vietnam (COSVN). Mr. Tho, who had an extensive knowledge of the VCI from many years as a PRU operative, thought these documents would likely be turned over to another courier in the An Tan free market for ultimate delivery to COSVN, which at the time was thought to be located near the Cambodian town of Kratie.

The only person who could identify this commo-liaison cadre was the source since he had actually been introduced to her previously by a village VC security cadre. The source only knew the party name of the commo-liaison cadre, not her real name, but he felt confident he could identify her if he saw her again. He described her as dark-complected, of average height and weight, approximately 45 years old, with her hair tied in a knot at the back of her neck. He thought she lived in a village on the southern border of Tay Ninh Province.

Considering the short time we had to act on this information, I took the arrest order that Mr. Tho had already drafted into the embassy house so I could show it to the POIC. The POIC, Charles O. Stainback, was an extremely intelligent and seasoned CIA veteran having spent many years in Afghanistan prior to coming to South Vietnam. He asked me only two questions. First, did I trust the

Capt Finlayson on the left with other Vietnamese and American members of the Tay Ninh Provincial reconnaissance Unit in garrison, in this case for the presentation of awards for bravery while supporting the U.S. Army 25th Infantry Division.

source of the information; and second, was I sure the source could identify the commo-liaison cadre if he saw her again? I told him Mr. Tho had confidence in the source since the source had provided valuable and accurate information in the past. I also told him that the source had stated he could identify the VCI in question because he had met her previously. This was good enough for the POIC, and he initialed the arrest order and instructed me to take it to the province chief immediately for his authorization to arrest this VCI courier.

As we turned to go, Mr. Stainback asked me how the PRU intended to arrest this commo-liaison cadre. I told him that it would not be a good idea to arrest her at her home, given that we probably could not locate her home in time, and besides, we needed to capture her with the enemy documents in her possession if we wanted to obtain any worthwhile intelligence and a conviction in court. I felt it was highly unlikely she would have the documents in her possession at her home. Mr. Tho had told me that Mr. Chinh, the chief of the Tay Ninh PRU, wanted to intercept this woman while she was actually traveling from her village to the An Tan Border Station and to use the source to identify her to a PRU capture team. The POIC agreed to this plan and instructed us to get the arrest order approved as quickly as possible.

Mr. Tho and I immediately drove my Toyota Jeep to the provincial headquarters in Tay Ninh City, a short five-minute ride from the embassy house, and walked into the outer office of the province chief, Colonel Thien, who we knew well and respected for his honesty and administrative ability. The province chief was very supportive of the PRU, but we all knew he took his job seriously, and he would not sign our arrest order unless we had our facts in order. If we failed to produce solid reasoning or evidence for an arrest, the province chief would likely disapprove the arrest order.

When we arrived at the provincial head-

quarters, we were ushered into Colonel Thien's office, where we quickly briefed him. We did not reveal the source of our information to him, and he did not want to know anyway. Instead, he asked us if we had evidence that this woman was indeed a VC commo-liaison cadre, and were we confident we could capture her without causing any harm to either her or any civilians in the immediate area of her capture. We stated that our source could provide definitive identification of the courier since he had met her before. We also told him that commo-liaison cadre seldom traveled with armed guerrillas as security, unlike other VCI, so we felt confident that we could capture her without violence of any kind.

At the Tay Ninh West Airbase prior to the launch of Operation Cliff Dweller II in November 1969. From left to right: Deputy PRU Chief Mr. Ngiem, Deputy PRU Advisor Sergeant First Class Robert Smith, USA, PRU Chief Mr. Chinh, and Captain Finlayson.
Photo courtesy of Col Andrew R. Finlayson

Mr. Tho stated that the PRU would take the source to a small drink shop near a bridge leading to the An Tan Border station, and when the source saw the commo-liaison cadre cross the bridge, he would signal the PRU by taking a towel from around his neck and putting it on his lap. A three-man PRU cell would be seated at another table in the drink shop or at an adjacent vegetable stall so they could easily see the source's signal yet not arouse suspicion. The PRU had borrowed a taxicab from a PRU family member, and they planned to use this cab to rapidly transport the prisoner once the arrest was made. Since the commo-liaison cadre had to walk across this small bridge to get to her final destination, the PRU felt very confident that she would not escape once she was identified. A second three-man PRU cell, also in civilian clothes and with hidden weapons, would be stationed at the intersection of Route 22 and the dirt road leading west to the An Tan Border Station to act as a security backup if the arrest did not go as planned and to help escort the prisoner after she was captured.

With the province chief's signature on the arrest order, we left the provincial headquarters and walked to the PRU headquarters and barracks located inside the same compound. There we met with Mr. Chinh and his deputy, Mr. Ngiem, and together we went over the plan for the capture of the commo-liaison cadre. Mr. Chinh planned to capture the VCI cadre using cells from the Tay Ninh City PRU team instead of the PRU Hieu Thien District team. Although the An Thanh Border Station was in Hieu Thien District and the PRU in that district knew the area quite well, he felt it would make for better operational security if PRU cells from outside the district were used since the capture team would be in place for several hours and most people in Hieu Thien, including the VC, knew the identities of the PRU in that district. He did not want anyone to recognize the members of the PRU cell making the arrest and possibly give warning to the VCI cadre before she crossed the bridge.

He also stressed the need to make the arrest at the bridge since it was a natural choke point and it was located in an area surrounded by rice paddies with few people in the vicinity aside from those people in a few shops near the bridge's west side. He ruled out any attempt to capture the VCI cadre at the An Tan Border Station because he knew that location was astride the Vietnamese-Cambodian border and a favorite meeting place of VC and NVA agents. They could quite easily hinder the arrest or attack the PRU cell before the prisoner could be transported to a safe location.

Once the plan was finalized, Mr. Chinh directed that the two PRU cells that were to conduct the operation be placed in isolation, meaning they would remain at the PRU headquarters until the operation was launched and would have no contact with anyone outside the PRU barracks, even family members. This was done to avoid any chance of the VC being tipped off by a possible penetration of the PRU. It was standard operating procedure for the Tay Ninh PRU to isolate teams before they were sent on a mission. They trusted their troops, but they made sure their operations were not compromised in any way.

Mr. Tho also took the arrest order to the Provincial Intelligence Operations Coordinating Committee (PIOCC) and briefed them that a PRU operation would be conducted the next day. He gave the PIOCC members the time and place of the operation so friendly forces would not interfere with its execution. The DIOCC in Hieu Thien district was also notified, and the Hieu Thien PRU team was alerted to stand by to assist the PRU cells from the city team if called upon.

Coordination with American and South Vietnamese units was essential to preclude friendly fire casualties, but it was also risky since we never knew if any of these friendly units had been penetrated by enemy agents. By launching our operations very shortly after notifying these units, we hoped that any enemy agents in these units would not have enough time to warn their colleagues.

All of the above actions were completed in just five hours on the day the target was identified. This rapid planning and approval process for a PRU operation was achieved because the Phoenix program was highly organized in Tay Ninh Province—each district maintained a fully operational DIOCC—and the PRU enjoyed the cooperation and support of the province chief. This cooperation was further aided by the positive reputation of the PRU among the Cao Dai religious community, which made up the bulk of the province's population and from which the majority of the Tay Ninh PRU members were drawn. Speed was a necessity because the Tay Ninh PRU knew from experience that intelligence was a very perishable commodity, and successful exploitation within 24 hours of receiving the intelligence was a major factor in a fruitful operation. Any longer than that and the intelligence often was of little use.

Early the next morning, before first light, the PRU capture cell left their barracks dressed in civilian clothes with their weapons hidden inside the taxicab. The source was picked up on the way to the operating area. The second PRU security cell and a radio operator drove a PRU Toyota three-quarter- ton truck south from the city to the intersection of Route 22 and the road leading west to the An Tan Border Station. My interpreter, Mr. Nguyen Hoang Lam, and I drove to the PRU compound at the headquarters of Hieu Thien District at Go Dau Ha to coordinate the operation with that district's DIOCC and to arrange for a PRU rapid reaction force if the capture operation went bad.

At approximately 1145, I received a radio call from the PRU security cell informing me that they had arrested the prisoner and all PRU members were on the way to the district headquarters. Thirty minutes later, the taxicab and the PRU truck drove into the district compound with the prisoner and a bag of oranges she had been carrying when she was captured. Rather than interrogating her at the district compound, we decided to imme-diately take her to the Provincial Interrogation Center (PIC) in Tay Ninh City for questioning.

At the PIC, she did not cooperate and stuck to her story that she was simply traveling to the An Tan Border Station free market to sell her oranges. She denied that she was a commo-liaison cadre or knew anything about the VC. The interrogation was conducted by a Vietnamese Special Branch interrogator assigned to the PIC with the American CIA PIC Advisor observing. Her story began to come apart when she was informed that she was positively identified by a witness and she could not explain the small scraps of coded paper she had secreted into two of the oranges she was carrying. She insisted the oranges came from her own trees and she had not inserted anything into them. She continued to be uncooperative, despite the evidence against her, and she was handed over to the Vietnamese National Police for trial. She later was convicted and sentenced to two years in jail. The documents she carried were sent to Saigon for decoding and exploitation.[34]

Conclusions

Without exception, every person interviewed for this book stated that they considered the PRU highly effective in defeating the VCI. The statistics for VCI captured and killed by the PRU are still classified by the CIA. Probably the most accurate open-source estimate of VCI killed and captured by the PRU from 1967 and 1972 is the figure cited in Mark Moyar's book, *Phoenix and the Birds of Prey*, which places the number between 700 and 1,500 per month for each month during those years.[35]

The author's experience in Tay Ninh Province during 1969 and 1970 tends to support Dr. Moyar's figures. During the eight months the author was a PRU advisor in Tay Ninh Province, his PRU killed or captured approximately 12 VCI per month. If extrapolated nationwide, this produces a figure of over 500 VCI eliminated per month by the PRU during the same eight months. Of course, aggregate numbers of VCI killed or captured were not necessarily the best indicator of "success" unless the aggregated losses far exceeded the ability of the enemy to replace his losses. We now know that the North Vietnamese were unable to replace the trained and experienced Southern VCI cadre at a rate that made up for the losses inflicted upon them by American and South Vietnamese forces. It was this inability to find suitable replacements for the VCI after Tet 1968 that convinced the North Vietnamese that they needed to change their strategy to one that did not rely on VC forces to achieve their objective of unifying all of Vietnam under their control. They recognized the pacification programs of the South Vietnamese were proving to be successful and any strategy that called for a "General Uprising" under the leadership of the southern wing of the Lao Dong Party was doomed to failure since both the number and quality of the VCI needed to accomplish this uprising were being systematically eroded by the Phoenix program. There was no more cogent proof of this than the actions taken by the North Vietnamese when they finally came to power in South Vietnam in 1975. In many provinces, the North Vietnamese victors found that too few VCI remained who could effectively administer the captured provinces. They had to resort to using sizeable numbers of Communist cadre sent to South Vietnam from North Vietnam just to provide basic governmental services.[36]

When the author asked the CIA and U.S. Marine advisors why they thought the PRU were so effective, they gave the following reasons:

• The PRU were *locally recruited* and, therefore, they had an intimate knowledge of their area of operations, the people living there, and the enemy they were fighting. As a local, the typical PRU soldier had years of experience in the province where he was employed, and he had a heightened sense of his surroundings that an outsider would not possess. Local knowledge made it easy for them to move at night and to move rapidly. It also facilitated the development of their organic intelligence system.

• The PRU had *strong leadership and discipline*. While not all PRUs had exceptional leaders for their chiefs and team leaders, most did, and this paid off handsomely in terms of unit cohesion, sustained personnel stability, and combat effectiveness. Most PRU chiefs and their team leaders were local men who enjoyed reputations for integrity, maturity, toughness, and intelligence. The Marine advisors often spoke highly of their PRU chiefs, their team leaders, and their interpreters and compared them favorably with the best combat leaders they had ever known. It follows that the recruitment of leaders for PRU-like units and their selection for advancement must be conducted with great care and consideration.

• PRU members were highly motivated due to the many VC atrocities they had witnessed and by the VCI attacks against their families. Many PRU members had experienced terrible crimes against their families by VC assassination squads, and these atrocities engendered in the PRU members a visceral hatred for the VCI. It is safe to say that the PRU were "true believers" who had clearly come to the conclusion that their very survival depended upon their ability to defeat the VCI completely. Efforts by the enemy to proselytize the PRU failed miserably.

• The PRU had *excellent organic intelligence systems*. Because of the problems with cooperation and coordination among the various U.S. and Vietnamese agencies involved with counter-VCI operations, the PRUs developed their own intelligence-gathering apparatus. The PRU undercover agents were usually unpaid informants, often family members, and, importantly, typically old women. They relied primarily on agents who did not have a financial interest in spying, but had a strong family or religious commitment to the PRU leadership and the defeat of the Communists.

53

Older women were more effective than any other PRU agent since they were able to move around their provinces more easily than men and could develop plausible stories for why they were in a certain area and asking questions.

Although most PRU operational leads were developed by their own organic intelligence system, they could on occasion benefit from other sources. Another very good source of intelligence for the PRU was information gleaned from the interrogation of VCI prisoners and VC who rallied to the government—the Hoi Chanhs. Many PRU were adept at recruiting former VC to provide information about the VCI in their villages, and some were even able to convince these former VC to return to their villages and spy on their former colleagues.

A third good source of operational leads, albeit one that required a great deal of labor-intensive data mining, was the maps created by the Census Grievance cadre, which identified the houses in each village by their political loyalty to the GVN. These color-coded maps that had houses marked in red as pro-VC or anti-GVN could, with much effort, produce valuable information on the VCI and their families. If the information on these Census Grievance maps had been digitized, they probably would have played a larger role in developing operational leads, but the amount of time-consuming research needed to analyze these maps made it less effective than it should have been.

Of course, had all of the DIOCCs functioned more effectively and had all the U.S. and Vietnamese entities involved with the fight against the VC cooperated and shared intelligence more freely, the need for the organic PRU intelligence systems would not have existed.

• The PRU network was very *diffi-cult for the enemy to penetrate* or recruit as spies because the PRU members had strong family, religious, and civic affiliations that were decidedly anti-Communist. Captured VCI and Hoi Chanhs confirmed the difficulty the enemy had penetrating the PRU during the Vietnam War, and they attributed this difficulty to the "political and social attitude" of the PRU members.

• There was little doubt in the minds of the Marine PRU advisors interviewed for this book that a very important element in the PRU's success was the fact that the PRUs were *organized, equipped, supplied, paid, and controlled by the CIA* and not the U.S. military. Before their assignment to the PRU, the U.S. advisors were used to the cumbersome command and control mechanisms used by the U.S. military to plan and launch operations. They were amazed when they were assigned to the CIA and saw how quickly decisions could by made by on-scene POICs for PRU operations. They were also used to the very paperwork-intensive and slow-moving logistics system that served the military in Vietnam, so they were equally amazed by the flexibility of the CIA's logistics system and the rapid way it responded to field requests by the PRUs for everything from transportation and uniforms to construction materials and ammunition.

The CIA way of doing business allowed the PRU advisors to concentrate on planning and conducting anti-VCI operations and not on tiresome and slow bureaucratic actions. PRU advisors enjoyed a great deal of autonomy and were left to use their own initiative in the field. They were not subject to having to report via radio to higher headquarters what their situation was or to file lengthy reports on every operation. In short, they were freed from the burdens that many other U.S. military personnel were subjected to, and this had a dramatic and positive impact on their ability to do their jobs properly.

Since the end of the Vietnam War, many writers, few of them with any firsthand knowledge of the PRU or the Phoenix program, have made outrageous claims about both. Most of these claims have been exposed as fraudulent, often made by people who were never assigned to the Phoenix program but claimed they were.[37] In fact, in the research done on this book, the author encountered one such person who claimed he had been a Marine advisor with the PRU when he clearly had not been.

The most pernicious claim has been that the Phoenix program was an out-of-control assassination program that killed innocent Vietnamese civilians in a profligate and indiscriminate manner. While there is no objective evidence to support such claims, they continue to persist, casting a dark cloud over the program and those associated with it. The U.S. PRU advisors and CIA officers who were interviewed by the author were asked directly if they were ever given a written or verbal order to assassinate anyone, VCI or otherwise, while they were assigned to the PRU. In every case, these former PRU advisors and CIA case officers were categorical in their denial that they had ever received such orders, with many adding that if they had, they would not have carried them out. They did receive orders to capture VCI, and often these attempts to capture VCI led to firefights and VCI deaths. Since most VCI traveled with armed guards or lived in VC-controlled or contested villages where VC guerrilla units provided protection to the VCI, it was highly likely that operations mounted to capture VCI would lead to violence and casualties on both sides.

In such cases, the PRU were well equipped and trained to handle such violent resistance. It is instructive to note that the Marines interviewed mentioned that most of their PRU casualties were the result of combined U.S. and joint ARVN military operations where the PRU were employed in a purely military role. It is also important to note that the Marine PRU advisors stated that they captured more VCI than they killed. U.S. PRU advisors and CIA officers were emphatic that the primary intent of the PRU anti-VCI operations was the capture of VCI so they could be interrogated and the intelligence gained from these interrogations exploited. Dead VCI were of no intelligence value to the PRU or the CIA, while every captured VCI was a potential double agent to be turned against the enemy or a source of valuable political intelligence.

Finally, the Marine PRU advisors stated that they received explicit instructions from Saigon that they were never to take any action that was in violation of the Uniform Code of Military Justice (UCMJ) and to report immediately any violation of the UCMJ by the PRU or any other unit they observed.[38] While it is impossible to say that no PRU member ever committed a violation of the UCMJ or the GVN laws concerning the rules of war, it can be stated emphatically that the policy of the MACV leadership and the CIA was abundantly clear on this issue: the PRUs and their U.S. advisors would take no action in violation of the UCMJ.

Lessons Learned

U.S. Marines have been involved in counterinsurgency operations throughout their history. From Central America, the Caribbean, and Vietnam in the 20th century to Iraq and Afghanistan in the 21st, the Marine Corps has been involved in combat against insurgents. One of the questions asked by the author in his interviews with the Marines who were PRU advisors was, "If you were confronted with an insurgency today, what lessons learned from your experiences with the PRU Program in Vietnam would you want to pass on to those who are assigned the difficult mission of defeating an insurgency?" The following lessons learned are a composite of their answers in terms of forming an organization similar to the PRU:

• **The units should be imbued with both a professional and civic ethos, one that makes them accountable to the people for their actions.** They should not be used by political leaders for partisan reasons, such as harassing local politicians from legally established political parties or providing assistance to further the interests of local commercial entities. They should be focused on one mission only—the defeat of the insurgency's political infrastructure.

• **They should be equipped and trained to a high level of professionalism.** One way to accomplish this is to establish organic logistics and training capabilities. The PRU had an excellent logistics system in the form of the CIA in-country logistics system, which the PRU advisors identified as superior to their own military logistics systems, especially in terms of rapid delivery of needed items and the lack of a cumbersome administrative and approval process. The mission of PRU-type units requires specialized training, so best results will be achieved if they have a training program specifically tailored to their needs.

• **They should be well paid and rewarded for tangible results.** The PRU were paid a salary each month, and they were also paid for captured weapons. Additionally, they received special monetary awards for high-level VCI captures. The fact that they were regularly paid and rewarded for superior results contributed in a very significant way to their very low desertion rates and the inability of the VCI to penetrate or proselytize them.

• **They should be organized into small, tightly knit teams whose ranks are filled with members from the communities they serve.** The fact that most PRU members were locally recruited was a key factor in their success. They knew the people and terrain in their area, and this local knowledge allowed them to move about freely and to develop an effective intelligence-gathering system. It also meant that their families often had well-established ties to the commercial and civic organizations in their provinces, a fact that contributed to their loyalty and dedication to their communities, as well as unit cohesion.

• **They should be subject to effective judicial and political oversight and not free to conduct missions without orders from a competent legal authority.** PRU-like units can be misused by corrupt government officials, so it is essential that mechanisms to ensure their proper employment are in place and rigorously imposed. Having the CIA in control of the PRU greatly diminished the capacity for corrupt South Vietnamese officials to misuse them.

• **They should not be given responsibility for the interrogation of captured prisoners beyond seeking perishable tactical information and holding them until transfer can be arranged.** Interrogations are far more effective when conducted by professional interrogators in facilities such as the Provincial and National Interrogation Centers that the CIA maintained during the Vietnam War. Untrained interrogators are often counterproductive, and the product of their interrogations can often result in false leads and unreliable intelligence.

• **There should be a clear separation between the PRU-type units and other police units, especially those involved in criminal investigations and arrests.** Using the specially trained units like the PRU for routine police work is a waste of a valuable asset and diminishes the high level of training required to execute PRU-like missions. PRU assets should never be diverted to other roles they are not trained or equipped for, such as military, executive protection, or static security missions.

• **The PRU-type units and their families must be protected from retribution and given assurances that their identities will not be revealed to the press or any other unauthorized source.** To do so makes them highly vulnerable to retribution by the enemy and causes them to worry about the safety of their families more than their mission. Consideration should be given to housing family members in secure compounds or locating them outside of the area where PRU-type units are stationed.

- **They should be provided with the highest level of professional and ethical leadership.** The PRU advisors were unanimous in their belief that there was a strong correlation between the leadership abilities of the Vietnamese PRU chiefs and team leaders and the effectiveness of the overall PRU program in their province. This means that the selection process for leadership positions must be based on an objective analysis of the character and abilities of the personnel selected for leadership positions, and this selection process should not be viewed as arbitrary by the rank and file.

- **They should be provided with full access to pertinent targeting intelligence through some mechanism similar to the South Vietnamese DIOCCs.** Most PRU advisors interviewed for this book stressed that their PRU was required to generate most operational leads through their own organic intelligence-gathering system and that the agencies represented on their respective DIOCCs did not regularly share operational leads worthy of exploitation. This is a key point when considering any counterinsurgency program. There must be cooperation and coordination between all the agencies involved in the counterinsurgency effort. No matter how good the organizational structure for combating the insurgency is, it will fail or be manifestly less effective unless there is acceptance at every level for the need to cooperate and coordinate.

- If U.S. military advisors are to be assigned to a PRU-like unit, they should possess the following characteristics and experience:

Rank. Since maturity and experience are needed for such duty, the PRU advisors and their CIA colleagues felt the optimum rank for an enlisted advisor should be that of E-7 (USMC gunnery sergeant) and for an officer O3 (USMC captain). In many cultures, the ability to interact effectively with your counterparts is determined by rank, so careful consideration should be given to this fact, if it applies.

Experience. PRU advisors were emphatic about the skill sets necessary for their jobs, and they identified experience in the infantry, ground reconnaissance, and intelligence fields as the most valuable.

Language Proficiency. Although most PRU advisors were not fluent in Vietnamese, they all stated that their jobs would have been much easier if they had possessed at least a basic fluency in that language, such as a score of 3/3 on the Department of Defense Language Proficiency Test. All too often, the PRU advisors were at the mercy of their interpreters, and this situation sometimes militated against their ability to exercise strong leadership and influence over their PRU counterparts. It was also a problem when PRU advisors went on operations with their units and the instantaneous response to orders was impeded by the need to have an interpreter translate orders and directions in a combat venue.

Cultural and Political Sensitivity. Simply possessing the military skills necessary to advise a PRU-like unit is often not enough. CIA officers felt PRU advisors needed to be culturally sensitive and politically knowledgeable in order to be fully effective. It helped if the PRU advisor understood the underlying dynamics of the people in his province, such as their history, religion, and civic relationships. Many PRU advisors had difficulty understanding the political influences in their provinces, and this sometimes led to misunderstandings about the proper role of their PRU teams. Some political sophistication on the part of the PRU advisor helped him bridge the gap between American and local perceptions about the proper way to pursue counterinsurgency goals and to find ways to avoid conflicts stemming from local political activity.

Training. The USMC advisors interviewed by the author had differing opinions on the training status of their respective PRU teams. Most considered their PRU team "well trained," and they spoke highly of the training that the PRU teams received at the CIA Vung Tau Training Facility in III Corps on the South China Sea.

Some advisors, however, identified serious training deficiencies in their units, especially in the areas of marksmanship, communications, and the use of supporting arms. Most USMC PRU advisors instituted local training programs to correct deficiencies and to maintain critical skills. They recommended that PRU-like units receive training in the following areas: marksmanship, small-unit tactics, raids, intelligence operations, staff planning, coordination of artillery and air support, first aid, scouting and patrolling, communications, military ethics, and the handling of prisoners to include field interrogation techniques. Since training was viewed as a critically important facet of the PRU's success, the advisors strongly recommended that all advisors have practical experience with these military skills or have formal training in the subjects before they are assigned to PRU-like duty.

Although not all U.S. Marine PRU advisors came from a reconnaissance background, the advisors felt Marines with ground reconnaissance experience were best suited for assignment to units similar to the PRU. The former PRU advisors also suggested that training for PRU-like units

should be done at a national-level facility devoted entirely to the subject matter needed for these specialized units. For security reasons and for continuity of effort, they felt all indigenous personnel assigned to operational units should be required to attend a basic course in the subjects mentioned above. They also recommended the creation of mobile training teams, which would be used for refresher training. This would free the advisor to concentrate on intelligence management and operational planning, instead of training.

Staff Planning. The duties of a PRU advisor required a demanding level of planning and coordination with friendly units. Since so many PRU operations involved raids, the PRU advisors felt a high level of competency in planning and rehearsing raids should be a requisite skill for any advisor. Although many PRU operations were conducted in a very short time after identifying a target, some took days or even weeks to plan and rehearse. In this regard, advisors should know how to prepare written orders for their operations and to ensure that these orders are coordinated with friendly units so as to avoid casualties from friendly fire. With this in mind, every PRU advisor should possess the knowledge of the rudimentary steps in staff planning and the ability to write clear and concise operational orders.

Personality Traits. As stated earlier, PRU advisors were often given a degree of autonomy by their CIA leaders that they would not normally be given in their military units. At times they were free to exercise their initiative with little supervision because their CIA bosses respected their expertise and judgment. "Special trust and confidence" was a term that was given great credence by the CIA POICs in their dealings with their Department of Defense assignees. Given the nature of their work and the level of autonomy granted them by their CIA bosses, the PRU advisors identified several character traits that should be considered when assigning military personnel to a PRU-like unit. They recommended that only personnel with maturity, patience, integrity, aggressiveness, and moral leadership be assigned to the independent duty of an advisor with a PRU-like unit.

Sources

In writing this work, the author wanted to rely as much as possible on primary sources—people with firsthand knowledge of the Marine Corps' contribution to the CIA's Provincial Reconnaissance Unit Program. The individuals listed below were either USMC PRU advisors or CIA officers who worked closely with the PRUs during the Vietnam War. Interviews were conducted by the author via numerous telephone calls and e-mails between January 2007 and June 2008 as additional questions were developed, points of clarification required, and memories strengthened. These interviews involved individuals who represented every level of PRU association, from the province level to the national level. Several former Vietnamese PRU members, now residing in the United States, were also interviewed by the author, but they wished to remain anonymous and the author respected their wishes.

Terence M. Allen

William Cervenak

Rudy Enders

Raymond R. Lau

Ronald J. Lauzon

Warren H. Milberg

Rodney H. Pupuhi

Douglas P. Ryan

Hank Ryan

Charles O. Stainback

Wayne W. Thompson

Frederick J. Vogel

Paul C. Whitlock

Bibliography

Ahern, Thomas L., Jr. *CIA and Rural Pacification in South Vietnam.* Langley, Va.: Center for the Study of Intelligence, Central Intelligence Agency, 2001.

Andrade, Dale. Ashes to Ashes: *The Phoenix Program and the Vietnam War.* Lexington, Mass.: Lexington Books, 1990.

----------, and James H. Willbanks. "CORDS/Phoenix: Counterinsurgency Lessons from Vietnam for the Future." *Military Review*, March-April 2006, 9-23.

Bass, Thomas A. *The Spy Who Loved Us: The Vietnam War and Pham Xuan An's Dangerous Game.* New York: Public Affairs, 2009.

Bergerud, Eric, M. *The Dynamics of Defeat: The Vietnam War in Hau Nghia Province.* Boulder, Colo.: Westview Press, 1991.

Berman, Larry. Perfect Spy: *The Incredible Double Life of Pham Xuan An, Time Magazine Reporter and Vietnamese Communist Agent.* New York: Smithsonian/Collins, 2007.

Burkett, B. G., and Donna Whitley. *Stolen Valor: How the Vietnam Generation was Robbed of Its Heroes and Its History.* Dallas, Verity Press, 1998.

Colby, William E., with James McCargar. *Lost Victory: A Firsthand Account of America's Sixteen-Year Involvement in Vietnam.* Chicago: Contemporary Books, 1989.

Corn, David. *Blond Ghost: Ted Shackley and the CIA's Crusades.* New York: Simon and Schuster, 1994.

Davidson, Phillip B. *Vietnam at War: The History, 1946-1975.* Novato, Calif.: Presidio Press, 1988.

Enders, Rudy. Unpublished manuscript. 2007.

Finlayson, Andrew R. "The Tay Ninh Provincial Reconnaissance Unit and Its Role in the Phoenix Program 1969-70." *Studies in Intelligence* 51-2 (2007): 59-69.

----------. "Vietnam Strategies." *Marine Corps Gazette*, August 1988, 90-94.

Karnow, Stanley. *Vietnam: A History.* New York: Viking, 1983.

Lau, Ray. "TET 1968." Unpublished manuscript. 2002.

Moyar, Mark. *Phoenix and the Birds of Prey: The CIA's Secret Campaign to Destroy the Viet Cong.* Annapolis, Md.: Naval Institute Press, 1997.

--------. Triumph Forsaken: *The Vietnam War, 1954-1965.* New York: Cambridge University Press, 2006.

--------. "Vietnam: Historians at War." *Academic Questions* 21 (March 2008): 37-51.

Pike, Douglas. *Viet Cong: The Organization and Techniques of the National Liberation Front of South Vietnam.* Cambridge, Mass.: Massachusetts Institute of Technology Press, 1966.

Plaster, John L. *SOG: The Secret Wars of America's Commandos in Vietnam.* New York: Onyx, 1997.

Pribbenow, Merle L. "The Man in the Snow White Cell." *Studies in Intelligence* 48-1 (2004): 45-58.

Race, Jeffrey. *War Comes to Long An: Revolutionary Conflict in a Vietnamese Province.* Berkeley: University of California Press, 1972.

Rodriguez, Felix I., and John Weisman. *Shadow Warrior: The CIA Hero of a Hundred Unknown Battles.* New York: Simon and Schuster, 1989.

Sorley, Lewis. *A Better War: The Unexamined Victories and Final Tragedy of America's Last Years in Vietnam.* New York: Harcourt Brace, 1999.

Sullivan, John F. Of Spies and Lies: *A CIA Lie Detector Remembers Vietnam.* Lawrence: University Press of Kansas, 2002.

Summers, Harry G. *On Strategy: The Vietnam War in Context.* Carlisle Barracks, Pa.: Strategic Studies Institute, U.S. Army War College, 1981.

U.S. Department of the Army. *The Communist Insurgent Infrastructure in South Vietnam: A Study of Organization and Strategy.* Department of Army Pamphlet 550-106. Washington, D.C.: Department of Army, March 1967.

Valentine, Douglas. The *Phoenix Program*. New York: Morrow, 1990.

Appendix
U.S. Marine Provincial Reconnaissance Unit Advisors

This is a tentative list compiled by the author from documents, from information supplied by surviving PRU Marines, and from names provided by Dr. Mark Moyar and Mr. Steve Sherman. As far as the author can determine, the last U.S. military PRU advisors left the program in early 1970.*

Allen, Terence M., Lieutenant Colonel, 20 February 1968 to 1 March 1970, National PRU
    Headquarters, Saigon

Below, Jack W., Staff Sergeant, 17 July 1967 to 13 January 1968, Regional Headquarters,
    I Corps, Da Nang, and Thua Thien Province, I Corps

Brause, Bernard B., Jr., Lieutenant Colonel, October 1968 to October 1969, Regional
    Headquarters, III Corps, Bein Hoa

Bright, Robert B., III, Sergeant, October 1966 to March 1967, Thua Thien Province,
    I Corps

Burlem, Ernest F. J., Gunnery Sergeant, September 1968 to May 1969, Quang Ngai Province,
    I Corps

Castaneda, Eugene, Sergeant, 17 July 1967 to 12 August 1967, Quang Tri Province, I Corps
    (Killed in Action)

Clark, James A., Captain, 3 November 1968 to 1 June 1969, Quang Tin Province,
    I Corps

Costa, John H., Gunnery Sergeant, January 1969 to August 1969, Thua Thien Province,
    I Corps

Coyle, Eugene R., Staff Sergeant, September 1969 to June 1970, Kien Tuong Province,
    IV Corps

Cox, George B., Jr., Staff Sergeant, September 1968 to May 1969, Thua Thien Province,
    I Corps

Croxton, Hoyt J., Jr., Staff Sergeant, May 1969 to February 1970, Rung Sat
    Special Zone

Davis, Bruce E., Captain, January 1969 to October 1969, Regional Headquarters,
    I Corps, Da Nang

Finlayson, Andrew R., Captain, October 1969 to June 1970, Tay Ninh Province,
    III Corps

---

*Felix Rodriguez was in charge of the PRU operations in III Corps in 1971. He did this largely by himself since the PRU advisors assigned by MACV were just about all gone by then and only a handful of contract CIA officers were assigned. He used U.S. military advisors to help him run his operations in III Corps, but these advisors were not PRU advisors and were not assigned to the CIA in any capacity.

Gardner, Joel R., First Lieutenant, 1967-1968, Khanh Hoa Province, II Corps
(Wounded in Action, evacuated)

Gray, James K., Staff Sergeant, September 1969 to April 1970, Binh Long Province,
III Corps

Gum, William E., Staff Sergeant, February 1969 to April 1969, Rung Sat Special Zone
(Wounded in Action, evacuated)

Harmon, Clyde E., Staff Sergeant, October 1968 to July 1969, Quang Ngai Province,
I Corps

Henrickson, Richard, Gunnery Sergeant, November 1968 to January 1970, Quang Nam
Province, I Corps

Hyslop, Kenneth D., Major, August 1969 to 20 September 1970, National PRU
Headquarters, Saigon

Jansen, Laurens J., Second Lieutenant, 9 July 1967 to October 1968, Regional Headquarters,
I Corps, Da Nang

Jarboe, Edmond J., Gunnery Sergeant, September 1969 to May 1970, Long An Province,
III Corps

Jones, Jack W., Staff Sergeant, June 1969 to December 1969, Vung Tau Training Center,
III Corps

Karkos, Norman, Sergeant, September 1968 to December 1968, Vung Tau Training Center,
III Corps

Kennedy, John V., Gunnery Sergeant, October 1968 to July 1969, Quang Tin Province,
I Corps

Kingrey, Robert N., Captain, August 1969 to October 1969, Quang Nam Province,
I Corps

Lauzon, Ronald J., Sergeant, 24 March 1967 to 8 October 1967, Thua Thien Province,
I Corps

Leach, Harold W., First Lieutenant, May 1968 to May 1969, Regional Headquarter,
I Corps, Da Nang

McAllister, Carlisle J., Gunnery Sergeant, June 1969 to July 1970, Kiang Giang Province,
IV Corps

Maher, Vincent F., Captain, October 1968 to August 1969, Binh Duong Province,
III Corps

Martin, William L., Staff Sergeant, 5 October 1968 to 24 June 1969, Quang Tin Province,
I Corps

Mayo, George O., Gunnery Sergeant, 7 May 1969 to 22 May 1969, Quang Ngai Province,
     I Corps (Killed in Action)

Meeker, Thomas H., Captain, 3 November 1968 to 3 August 1969, Thua Thien Province,
     I Corps

Molnar, Ronald F., Sergeant, 18 March 1968 to 18 December 1968, Quang Nam Province,
     I Corps

Necaise, Gerald I., Gunnery Sergeant, May 1969 to July 1969, Quang Tin Province,
     I Corps

Perice, Carl D., Sergeant, 16 March 1968 to 20 December 1968, Thua Thien Province,
     I Corps

Polchow, William A., Sergeant, unknown start to 23 January 1968, Quang Nam Province,
     I Corps (Killed in Action)

Prater, Gerald W., Staff Sergeant, September 1969 to January 1970, Quang Tin Province,
     I Corps

Pupuhi, Rodney H., Sergeant, 11 March 1968 to 16 December 1968, Quang Nam Province,
     I Corps

Purlem, Ernest F., Gunnery Sergeant, 13 September 1968 to 24 May 1969, Quang Ngai
     Province, I Corps

Rich, James D., Sergeant, 6 July 1967 to 14 November 1967, Thua Thien Province,
     I Corps

Robinson, Leland M., Sergeant, 28 February 1968 to 28 September 1968, Quang Tin
     Province, I Corps

Ryan, Douglas P., First Lieutenant, 13 October 1968 to 30 July 1969, Regional Headquarters,
     I Corps, Da Nang; Quang Tin and Quang Tri Provinces, I Corps

Shields, Rodney P., Corporal, 15 January 1968 to 20 November 1968, Quang Ngai Province,
     I Corps

Stepro, Allen D., Staff Sergeant, 30 October 1968 to 8 July 1969, Bien Hoa Province,
     III Corps (Wounded in Action, evacuated)

Tafaoa, Fitu, Staff Sergeant, November 1968 to May 1969, Quang Nam Province,
     I Corps, and Vung Tau Training Center, III Corps

Thompson, Wayne W., Staff Sergeant, 9 July 1967 to March 1968, Quang Tin Province,
     I Corps

Vaughn, Howard G., Sergeant, 1967 to 3 February 1968, Thua Thien Province,
     I Corps (Killed in Action)

Vialpando, Herman P., Staff Sergeant, 9 July 1967 to August 1967, (no province indicated on orders), IV Corps (Wounded in Action, evacuated)

Vogel, Frederick J., Captain, February 1969 to September 1969, Quang Nam Province, I Corps

Watkins, Lee H., Staff Sergeant, 8 July 1967 to 1 January 1968, Quang Ngai Province, I Corps

Whitlock, Paul C., Staff Sergeant, December 1966 to June 1967, Quang Tri Province, I Corps

Williams, Roderick D., Gunnery Sergeant, April 1969 to October 1969, Quang Ngai Province, I Corps

Yorck, David C., Captain, August 1969 to September 1970, Regional Headquarters, Bein Hoa, III Corps

Endnotes

1. Mark Moyar, *Phoenix and the Birds of Prey* (Annapolis, Md.: Naval Institute Press, 1997), 346-65; see also Dale Andrade, *Ashes to Ashes: The Phoenix Program and the Vietnam War* (Lexington, Mass.: Lexington Books, 1990), 185-88; John F. Sullivan, *Of Spies and Lies: A CIA Lie Detector Remembers Vietnam* (Lawrence: University Press of Kansas, 2002), 118-21.

2. Throughout this book, the U.S. Marine Corps (USMC) personnel assigned to the PRU Program are called "advisors," but this is technically incorrect, especially for those Americans assigned before November 1969, when Military Assistance Command, Vietnam (MACV) Headquarters changed the title of the U.S. military assigned to the PRU from "commander" to "advisor." At this same time, MACV ordered these American military personnel to no longer accompany the PRU teams on operations. Despite this change in policy, there was no doubt in the minds of the PRU teams who their commander was. There was no doubt who gave the orders, who paid them, and who equipped them—it was the American assigned to them. Unlike other American advisors to South Vietnamese military forces, the Americans assigned to the PRUs were both doctrinally and factually in command of their units.

3. Mark Moyar, *Triumph Forsaken: The Vietnam War, 1954-1965* (New York: Cambridge University Press, 2006); Lewis Sorley, *A Better War: The Unexamined Victories and Final Tragedy of America's Last Years in Vietnam* (New York, Harcourt Brace, 1999); Harry G. Summers, *On Strategy: The Vietnam War in Context* (Carlisle Barracks, Pa.: Strategic Studies Institute, U.S. Army War College, 1981); Andrew R. Finlayson, "Vietnam Strategies," *Marine Corps Gazette*, August 1988, 90-94.

4. Rudy Enders, e-mail to author, 11 July 2008.

5. Mark Moyar, "Vietnam: Historians at War," *Academic Questions* 21 (March 2008): 40-43.

6. Larry Berman, *Perfect Spy: The Incredible Double Life of Pham Xuan An,* Time *Magazine Reporter and Vietnamese Communist Agent* (New York: Smithsonian/Collins, 2007), 137. For additional sources on Communist verification of the effectiveness of the Phoenix program, see Dale Andrade and James H. Willbanks, "CORDS/Phoenix Counterinsurgency Lessons from Vietnam for the Future," *Military Review*, March-April 2006, 21.

7. Douglas Valentine, *The Phoenix Program* (New York: Morrow, 1990), 166-67.

8. Felix I. Rodriguez and John Weisman, *Shadow Warrior* (New York: Simon and Schuster, 1999), 189-93; David Corn, *Blond Ghost: Ted Shackley and the CIA's Crusades* (New York: Simon and Schuster, 1994), 291.

9. Terence M. Allen, telephone interview with author, 26 June 2008.

10. Andrade, *Ashes to Ashes*, 87-88; Andrew R. Finlayson, "The Tay Ninh Provincial Reconnaissance Unit and Its Role in the Phoenix Program, 1969-70," *Studies in Intelligence* 51-2 (2007): 66-67.

11. Rudy Enders, unpublished manuscript, 3-4.

12. Moyar, *Phoenix and the Birds of Prey*, 167.

13. Ibid., 167-69; Valentine, *Phoenix Program*, 167.

14. Finlayson, "Tay Ninh PRU," 66.

15. Warren H. Milberg, e-mail to author, 19 July 2008. Milberg, a CIA officer, was assigned to Quang Tri Province in 1967 and was the senior CIA official there. He was responsible for bilateral intelligence operations with the South Vietnamese in that province and, as part of that assignment, he was the supervisor of the USMC military PRU advisor.

16. Rodney Pupuhi, letter to author, 12 February 2008, author's possession.

17. The tactical advantages that accrued to PRU teams on operations when they were wearing enemy uniforms and using enemy weapons was cited by Ronald J. Lauzon and Rodney Pupuhi in telephone interviews with the author on 15 January and 7 February 2008, respectively.

18. John L. Plaster, *SOG: The Secret Wars of America's Commandos in Vietnam* (New York: Onyx, 1997), 133-37; Warren H. Milberg, e-mail to author, 19 July 2008.

19. During telephonic interviews and in e-mails, Ronald J. Lauzon, Paul C. Whitlock, Rodney H. Pupuhi, and Frederick J. Vogel mentioned the varied use of public and private means of transportation by the PRU for operations in their provinces.

20. The author believed having the signature of the province chief on each arrest order, as well as that of the provincial magistrate, gave his PRU the political and legal protection needed for the PRU to make a capture. Without these signatures on the arrest order, the PRU could later be accused of making an arbitrary capture.

21. Rudy Enders, e-mail to author, 20 June 2008.

22. Paul Whitlock, e-mails to author, 20 and 28 June 2008.

23. Rudy Enders, e-mail to author, 5 July 2008.

24. William R. Redel was a CIA officer who wore a Marine colonel's uniform. Valentine, *Phoenix Program*, 166-67.

25. Ronald Lauzon, letter to author, 7 February 2008, author's possession.

26. Wayne Thompson, interview with author, 28 July 2008.

27. Joel Gardner, e-mail to author, 17 November 2008.

28. Terence M. Allen, letter to author, 11 July 2008, author's possession.

29. Ray Lau, "The TET Offensive" (typescript, 2002).

30. This individual was probably CIA officer William Redel who often introduced himself as a Marine colonel and wore a Marine colonel's uniform.

31. Rodney Pupuhi, letter to author, 7 February 2007, author's possession.

32. Douglas P. Ryan, e-mail to author, 19 April 2008.

33. Frederick Vogel, e-mail to author, 18 April 2008.

34. Author's notes and memory, drawing from PRU Monthly Activity Report, March 1970, in author's possession.

35. Moyar, *Phoenix and the Birds of Prey*, 173.

36. Author interviews conducted in 1985 with two former Tay Ninh PRU who had escaped from Vietnam in 1983 and relocated to the United States. There is probably no stronger confirmation of the success of the Phoenix program than the statements made by the foremost Viet Cong spy, Pham Xuan An, to journalist Thomas A. Bass in 2007, in which he noted the efficiency of the Phoenix program in neutralizing the opposition in the South after the Tet Offensive. Thomas A. Bass, *The Spy Who Loved Us: The Vietnam War and Pham Xuan An's Dangerous Game* (New York: Public Affairs, 2009), 253.

37. Rudy Enders, e-mail to author, 18 April 2008. For a comprehensive and devastating critique of these fraudulent claims, see B. G. Burkett and Donna Whitley, *Stolen Valor: How the Vietnam Generation was Robbed of Its Heroes and Its History* (Dallas, Verity Press, 1998).

38. The author received verbal orders to comply with the Uniform Code of Military Justice and the Geneva Convention on the treatment of prisoners of war on two separate occasions. The first was during his initial briefing at the PRU Headquarters in Saigon with Lieutenant Colonel Terence

M. Allen in late September 1969. The second was during a staff visit by Major Kenneth D. Hyslop, USMC, in Tay Ninh City in early October 1969. He was also told by Charles O. Stainback, the Tay Ninh POIC, to obtain written concurrence with this policy from the chief of the Tay Ninh PRU, Mr. Chinh, and to cosign this document on 30 October 1969. All PRU chiefs and their advisors were required to sign these concurrence documents.

Made in the USA
Coppell, TX
23 June 2022